HANNAH
25
25
25

HURRICANE!

THE BOB HANNAH STORY

by Tom Madigan

motorbooks

DEDICATION

Hurricane! The Bob Hannah Story is dedicated to: Sweet T, Red, Wild Bill, and Ashley the Wonder Dog.

The sands of time flow smoothly, but
Ever so quickly, through the hourglass
Of life.

Ashley the Wonder Dog was part of the Hannah inner circle. A gift from his sister Tammy, Ashley was Bob's copilot, hunting partner, and sidekick. Ashley was one of the greatest dogs ever. *TMP*

First published in 2008 by Motorbooks, an imprint of MBI Publishing Company, 400 First Avenue North, Suite 300, Minneapolis, MN 55401 USA

Library of Congress Cataloging-in-Publication Data

Madigan, Tom, 1938-
Hurricane! : the Bob Hannah story / Tom Madigan.
p. cm. -- (Motor mania)
ISBN 978-0-7603-3300-6 (hb w/ jkt)
1. Hannah, Bob. 2. Motorcyclists—United States—Biography. 3. Motocross—United States. 4. Motorcycle racing—United States. I. Title.
GV1060.2.H34M23 2008
796.7'5092—dc22
[B]

2008025681

On the cover: Bob Hannah on the Yamaha 125cc bike he rode his first year as a factory racer. *Courtesy of Dick Miller; Racer X Illustrated Archives*

On the frontispiece: Due to his success on the track, Bob Hannah was among the first motocross riders to sport sponsor endorsement logos on his apparel. In this photo, taken in 1979, you can see the DG Performance logo on his helmet between his trademark lightning bolts. DG was his first sponsor. *Dennis Kanegae*

On the title pages: The Hurricane gets some air at the 1985 AMA 250cc Nationals at Hangtown in California. *TMP*

On the back cover, main: Look closely at the riding style of the Hurricane during a 125cc Outdoor National at Saddleback Park in 1982. Every time the subject of riding style was brought up, Hannah would always say that riders like Bailey and O'Mara had style; he would simply hang on no matter what happened. *Larry Maiers*

Bottom left: Although Hannah ran in Europe several times during his career, he never really cared for the place. He missed his home in Idaho and could not get used to the food. In 1978 he was part of the U. S. team at Gaildorf Germany during the running of the Motocross des Nations. *Terry Good*

Bottom right: Known for years as "Buckwheat" to his friends, Hannah changed his logo to "Wheat" in 1987 when he was riding for Suzuki. The reason remains unknown, but some speculate it was rooted in political correctness. *TMP*

Editor: James Manning Michels
Designer: Cindy Laun
Jacket Designer: Claire MacMasters

Printed in Hong Kong

CONTENTS

FOREWORD	By Roger DeCoster	**6**
PROLOGUE		**8**
INTRODUCTION		**10**
CHAPTER 1	Hillclimbing, Eating Pucker Bushes, Satan's Slaves, and Catalina Island	**20**
CHAPTER 2	Minibikes, Bunny Hopping, and Never Eating Dirt	**26**
CHAPTER 3	Weather Alert: Hurricane Gathering on the Horizon	**38**
CHAPTER 4	In the Eye of the Storm: Friends and Memories	**58**
CHAPTER 5	Hurricane Watch: Eyewitness Accounts from a Reporter on the Scene	**104**
CHAPTER 6	The Good Times	**126**
CHAPTER 7	WFO in the Afterlife of Motocross	**150**
CHAPTER 8	The Long Beach Celebrity Fiasco	**162**
CHAPTER 9	No More Starting Gates: Living Happily Ever After	**168**
EPILOGUE	A Few Last Words from the Professor	**172**
INDEX		**174**
ACKNOWLEDGMENTS		**176**

FOREWORD

Five-time World Motocross Champion Roger DeCoster is one of the greatest motocross riders in the history of the sport. When he competed on the world scene, his style was perfection in motion. He was aggressive, fast, fearless, and always charging to the lead. For the last four years of his fantastic career, DeCoster battled furious duels in the dirt with Bob Hannah on American and European tracks. Both riders were tough and rough, and neither gave an inch to the other. Both felt they would win every time the starting gate dropped. Although each man respected the other, on the track they considered themselves enemies.

Over time, they found their way onto the same team and therefore were pledged to the same goal: win at all costs.

When this book was conceived, Bob Hannah said he would be honored if Roger would consent to expressing a few words in reflection. Here, then, are those words.

ROGER DECOSTER

When I was asked to write the foreword to this book, I felt simultaneously honored and worried. How I could write something well enough to express my feelings about Bob Hannah?

Bob was certainly one of the toughest competitors I faced during my racing career. Not only was Bob fit and extremely motivated, he was very outspoken, much like the great boxing champion Muhammad Ali. And like Ali, Bob backed up his words with action. He would hang it out whenever and however much was needed and, amazingly, he'd find a way to stay on the bike—no matter how incredible the situation. And on those rare occasions where Bob did actually come off the bike, being as quick and agile as a cat, he would get right back on and moving again, rarely losing any ground in the process.

After I retired as a racer and was working with my friend and ex-teammate Dave Arnold, we decided to hire Bob to join David Bailey and Johnny O'Mara at Team Honda. For the first time, I had the opportunity to work with Bob instead of having to go out and try and beat him. At first, because of his intensity and drive, it was hard to keep things smooth inside the team. Then Bob had a terrible accident and everything changed. While on the sidelines during his long rehab waiting for his return to racing, he became an instrumental part of the team and its overall success. All things considered, in my eyes Bob was the professional's professional.

Although I could not admit it or tell anyone about it while I was still racing against him, I always had a tremendous amount of respect for Bob Hannah. And after all these years, I still do.

Roger DeCoster
2008

Above: One of the greatest names in the world of motocross racing is five-time world champion Roger DeCoster. While riding for Team Suzuki at the end of his riding career, he and Yamaha-mounted Hannah were bitter enemies who shared a mutual respect. *Steve Reyes*

After years of battle on tracks around the world, Roger DeCoster and Bob Hannah ended up on the same team. DeCoster, while managing Team Honda, hired Hannah after he left Yamaha. *Steve Reyes*

Roger DeCoster admitted that he respected Bob Hannah, but never really said anything to him directly. When Roger consented to writing the foreword to this book, he put his feelings into words. *Steve Reyes*

Bitter rivals during Hannah's early days with Yamaha, Dave Arnold and his rider Marty Smith battled Bob Hannah and Bill Buchka for the 1976 125cc Outdoor National Championship, with Hannah taking the title. In 1983, Arnold and Roger DeCoster hired Hannah for Team Honda. Shown here in 1985, Arnold and Bob confer at the Washougal, Washington, 250cc Outdoor Nationals. *TMP*

PROLOGUE

The Hurricane on his Honda in the 250cc Outdoor National at Hangtown in 1985. *Steve Reyes*

Any story, regardless of length, content matter, or language, needs only three elements to be understood and enjoyed: There must be a beginning, a pinnacle, and a conclusion. Other components, such as style, choice of viewpoint, and accuracy of facts are left to individual interpretation. So it is with the Bob Hannah story.

While writing this book, I faced several rather daunting challenges. The first, and biggest, challenge came from the fact that even though I have been writing about and attending racing events for more than forty years, most of that time has been spent in the world of automobile racing, not motorcycle racing. In fact, there was a time before which motocross racing was completely outside my realm of experience. I would have to be very cautious in my approach to telling this story so as not to embarrass myself or Bob Hannah with a final product that, when exposed to experts in the field, would contain inaccuracies.

The second challenge I faced was selecting from the many stories naturally created by a person so colorful and accomplished as Bob Hannah. How could I include the hundreds of fantastic races Hannah rode, or allow all of his countless friends to offer their comments, or satisfy the desire for insight accrued by the millions of fans Hannah had accumulated throughout his incredible career? The simple and direct answer to these questions was that it would be impossible. No single volume of work could package completely the accomplishments of someone of Hannah's stature. The solution was to choose major events from the Hannah saga and use these milestones to present an understanding of his daring deeds. As Hannah told me, "There are what I call 'critical points' in my career that allowed me to continue advancing. I want them to be recognized as key points in this story."

After much consideration and many sleepless nights, I made my decision as to how the task would be accomplished. Since it was the Bob Hannah story, much of the text should come from Hannah's own words, thoughts, and memories. And because I have spent nearly thirty years as his friend, I deemed myself eligible as a witness. I not only covered many of the major races during the final three years of Bob's career, writing pages of notes and shooting hundreds of photos, I also experienced firsthand some of his most challenging life moments, so we both felt comfortable allowing a portion of this book's content to come from my own bank of memories. Finally, to fill in the blanks, several close friends and loved ones would be called upon to offer their testimony to what they experienced during Bob's career.

Once these three elements were in place, I was ready. The story would begin in the desert of Southern California, as a little boy learned to ride a minibike. It would reach its pinnacle when the boy grew to manhood and achieved fame and fortune. It would end only after life presented challenges that tested the mettle of a champion's inner soul—and would not be complete until he proved he would not relent until all his goals were achieved.

The story is now ready to be told. All who read it will learn what can be accomplished with determination, grit, desire, and commitment.

Motocross racing requires endurance, skill, determination, and the ability to overcome a little mud. *Steve Reyes*

Brian Lunniss once remarked that the Los Angeles Supercross race had never been kind to Hannah and his Honda. Things didn't change much in 1986, when the Hurricane ran the event mounted on a Suzuki. *TMP*

It was agreed that Boyko would bring Hannah to my home for a meeting. Boyko, an outgoing and charismatic personality, was all smiles as he presented a then nineteen-year-old Hannah to me and Darlene, my wife. The young man was quite shy, and it seemed apparent that he was very uncomfortable meeting new people. After some discussion, I agreed to try and explore the possibility of a ride in a single-seat racing buggy. No promises. I looked at the situation as a one-time event and figured that, no matter the outcome, I would probably not have much to do with the young rider after this encounter. Nothing could have been further removed from the eventual reality.

I knew Baja very well, having pre-run races with the likes of Parnelli Jones, Walker Evans, Roger Mears, and Steve McQueen. Racing in Baja is a very lonely and dangerous experience; this is magnified tenfold if you are a rookie. At that time, Baja racing was still an activity with few spectators and poor radio communications; if you crashed hard, you were on your own until someone, usually a fellow racer or chase crew, found you. Since I didn't know much about his abilities as a racer, I was not very confident about young Bob Hannah's chances in Baja. That changed shortly before the Baja race was run.

In July, at the invitation of Ken Boyko and Gary Harlow, I had the opportunity to watch Hannah race a Supercross event at the Los Angeles Coliseum. I decided to go and check out firsthand whether the skinny kid could live up to his press clippings.

The Los Angeles Coliseum had been the site of many historic events, from the Olympics in 1932 to midget auto racing after World War II. But on the night I went, it was to witness a new phenomenon called Supercross, created by an extroverted promoter named

Riders like Jimmy Ellis rode hard and laid the groundwork for riders to come, including the Hurricane. Many of the pioneers of motocross in the United States never received the recognition they deserved. *Steve Reyes*

At the 1978 Motocross des Nations, the Hurricane rode for the United States and Yamaha on an OW39 500cc bike. It was a departure from his usual 250cc ride, upon which he won the '78 National Championship and the Supercross Championship. *Moto Verte; Terry Good*

Mike Goodwin. As night fell and the lights of the giant stadium began to blaze, the shy, skinny kid I had met earlier was now in his own element—and he seemed to be the focus of most everyone's attention.

Because I was a member of the working press, I garnered track credentials and, therefore, was within a few feet of the starting gate. As I gazed into the grandstands, I saw a boiling cauldron of motorcycle zealots, seemingly all clad in a garish array of hats, shirts, and jackets ablaze with logos identifying their allegiance to one of the gladiators now poised to do battle.

As the engines fired up, I suddenly found myself caught up in the action. My attention was directed to a character who seemed to be straight out of Central Casting, complete with tuxedo and ruffled shirt. His name was Larry Huffman, a.k.a "Supermouth," and, as

While sitting out the 1980 season as his broken leg healed, Hannah took up flying. In 1982, he bought a Cessna 210 and invited me to take a ride. Here, two friends have a good laugh after a bumpy flight from Thousand Oaks, California, to Hailey, Idaho. *TMP*

the announcer, his goal was to incite the crowd into a state of hysteria. Huffman began screaming at the fans, the way a fire-and-brimstone preacher might while attempting to save his flock from damnation.

The sound of twenty two-stroke motorcycles at full rpm coupled with the rantings of a madman brought a strange sensation to the back of my neck. The starting gate dropped and mayhem broke loose. The first turn was a spectacle of drama, as the twenty riders all dove for a patch of dirt barely able to offer room enough for one. Hannah was knocked to the ground in the first-turn chaos but managed to gather his senses together and take off after the pack. Within minutes, my whole image of this young man changed completely. As if possessed by a demon, Hannah flew over jumps, careened through corners, and defied gravity as he began to pick off competitors one by one. And all the while Hannah was cutting riders down, Supermouth was whipping the fans into a frenzy with his continuous shriek of "HERE COMES HANNAH!"

Hannah crashed that night before he could take the lead, but I had seen enough. Here was someone who equaled the raw courage and determination of any car racer I had ever known. In fact, that night I placed Hannah in the same category as three car racers whose grit and insatiable passion for winning I had witnessed firsthand: A. J. Foyt, Dale Earnhardt Sr., and my close friend Parnelli Jones. I would find out later just how profoundly true this assessment of Hannah would prove to be.

During that first racing encounter, I discovered several deeply rooted elements to the Hannah persona. I found most competitors didn't like him. The fans were divided, and so was the press. He would not go out of his way to give interviews, nothing but first place ever interested him, and his intense nature made those who didn't know him avoid his path. There was no gray area in his personality; it was either black or it was white.

During the late 1970s, Bob Hannah was the undisputed king of American motocross, winning seven championships and countless races in the United States and Europe. He had started with nothing and made himself into a world-renowned sports figure. He was on top. Then, in 1979, the world of the Hurricane changed forever.

While water-skiing, Hannah's leg was shattered—broken in sixteen places. There was talk of amputation. Questions surfaced: Was his career over? Would he lose the leg? Would the Hurricane ever ride a motorcycle again?

During his long rehabilitation period, Hannah visited my home in California on a regular basis, using it as a place to stay while undergoing treatment and therapy. It was a time of reflection for Hannah, and some of his priorities shifted. Airplanes became a new challenge for him. He bought his first plane, a Piper 250 Comanche, from a friend of mine named Vic Hickey. Hickey, who sold the plane on the merits of its exterior appearance, but under the skin things were not as good as they could have been. After spending a large sum of money to get the plane into flying condition, Hannah reminded me I should be more careful when recommending the purchase of a machine that, even when working properly, could kill its owner.

Looking for something to do in 1980 while rehabbing his injured leg, Bob again began to look at four-wheel off-road racing. Mickey Thompson got Hannah a ride in a single-seat buggy with a team operated by Tracy Valenta, who owned a company called Tracy Party Ice, which supplied ice machines to major grocery markets and convenience stores. The team Valenta sponsored included well-known drivers Rick and Roger Mears. It was agreed that Hannah would try his luck at the Mexican 1000, a race usually held in November. The agreement was made in June, so there would be time for both Valenta and Hannah to change their minds. But both parties were game, and the deal held.

By the time his race in Baja arrived, I had gotten to know Hannah on a slightly more personal level, so I tried to provide him with as much input about the race as I could. As Hannah climbed into the Tracy Party Ice single-seat Unlimited Class One racing buggy, I was somewhat worried about his chances of getting very far down the course. However, although he had not had an opportunity to pre-run the course as did the rest of the field, he had already driven a buggy of this caliber in competition.

As the race unfolded, Hannah not only drove the buggy like he stole it, but he ran to the front of the pack. Down the course, pit-crew radio transmissions

Above and next two pages: In 1986, as a result of making a motorcycle-safety film for the United States Navy, Bob Hannah was invited to fly with the Blue Angels. Although by that time Hannah had been flying his own Pitts Special Aerobatic plane in competition, after his flight with the Angels he remarked, "Those guys humbled me." *TMP*

crackled and spotter planes reported that Hannah was running hard and going for the lead. Shock waves penetrated the field and some competitors resented this rookie challenging their race. Rumors (although never substantiated) spread that some drivers resorted to using their own secret shortcuts to stay ahead of this newcomer. His audacity couldn't last; Baja itself would not allow an outsider to win. Indeed, Hannah's buggy broke a half axle, but he was able to make repairs and finished a remarkable fourth, just behind behind many-time winner Malcolm Smith.

As the years passed, Bob became my close friend. In the course of documenting Hannah's career, I attended many Supercross and AMA Outdoor National motocross events with my wife, shooting photos and taking notes. Although his leg healed and he regained his championship form, his ability to avoid injury—as he had prior to his skiing accident—failed him. On several occasions, crashes left him battered and bruised, and one in particular came close to again putting an end to his career. He moved from Yamaha to Honda, and then to Suzuki. Hannah matured from wild young

BLUE ANGELS

man to businessman to AMA Motorcycle Hall of Fame champion to motocross racing legend. And, as is the case in any pack of predators, the young guns of motocross wanted to catch the Hurricane and prove themselves equal.

Finally, in 1989, at one of his favorite tracks, Unadilla, New York, Bob Hannah retired from motocross racing. He then made a brief foray into open-wheel racing, but found his new calling in flying and racing airplanes. With the same style he showed in motocross, Hannah took on the dangers of flying a P-51 Mustang at 500 miles per hour and only fifty feet off the ground by using pure determination and courage.

By the 1990s, airplanes were Bob's business and motocross racing was history. I actually asked Hannah to consider writing a book in 1990, but he was not ready, saying, "I don't care about reliving the past." In 2007, I asked again and he relented. I would not refer to his decision as mellowing out; he just said yes.

In the thirty-odd years I have known Bob Hannah, I have learned some cold, hard facts about this many-time champion. During his career, winning was everything; second place was equal to a DNF as far as he was concerned. His personal space is his own; trespassers are not allowed. He is a very serious person whenever money is involved. He is not afraid to take a position on questions of right and wrong. He will not tolerate lying, cowardliness, weakness, or insincerity. He will never turn his back on a friend.

The Bob Hannah story, as we shall see, is one of grit and self-determination.

When Bob Hannah was inducted into the Motorsports Hall of Fame in 2000, his Yamaha mechanic Keith McCarty (right) and track announcer Larry Maiers (left) attended. Both men played important roles in the Hurricane's career—McCarty as his Yamaha mechanic and Maiers as the voice who could whip a crowd into a "Hannah, Hannah" chant at any given moment. *Hannah*

The Catalina Grand Prix, held on tiny Catalina Island twenty-six miles off the shore of Long Beach, opened the door for motorcycle racing to grow. It was partly from that beginning that motocross racing picked up the interests of enthusiasts. *Catalina Island Museum*

1

HILLCLIMBING, EATING PUCKER BUSHES, SATAN'S SLAVES, AND CATALINA ISLAND

In the United States, the early days of motocross racing featured motorcycle manufacturers with names like Norton, Greeves, Husqvarna, Bultaco, and (shown here) CZ. By today's standards, the early bikes were heavy and very hard to handle. *Steve Reyes*

When motocross first became popular in the United States, many of the superstars came from Europe. One of the best European riders was Gerrit Wolsink, teammate of Roger DeCoster, on Team Suzuki. *Steve Reyes*

In 1966, a Husqvarna importer named Edison Dye got the idea of bringing the 250cc World Champion motocross rider Torsten Hallman to ride several exhibition races in the United States. It was the first time America was exposed to a high level of motocross racing and to a lightweight bike like the Husky. It was a cool promotion idea for Husqvarna. In 1967, Edison came back with not just Torsten but a group of European riders who made coming to America an off-season adventure. Guys like Joel Robert and Gunnar Lindstrom came over for fun. The great thing about this period was that not only did the great riders of Europe come to the United States, but they brought their bikes. A rider like myself, living in California, I had never seen a CZ, Husky, Maico, Greeves, or a Bultaco, let alone ride one. We were pumped and didn't want places like Pepperell and Grafton in Massachusetts to have all the fun; we wondered when motocross would hit California.

It didn't take long before the promoters saw the light and realized that if they paid European riders to show up, they could draw a crowd. And Southern California was the perfect place to hold any kind of racing event.

I remember one day someone told me that they were going to run a motocross race at a place called Hopetown or Corriganville; it was a movie ranch/scrambles track owned by Bob Hope. The way I understood things, a famous Southern California motorcycle club called the Dirt Diggers was putting on a motocross race and Torsten Hallman was going to be there, ready to race any American who wanted to challenge him. I went, figuring that I had always held my own in scrambles and TT events, I made a few bucks racing flat track, so why not take a shot at motocross? I got a lesson I would never forget. It would not be fair to say I raced at Hopetown; Torsten was on a Husky and I was on a 650cc Triumph.

Later in 1967, Edison Dye came up with an idea for a series called the Inter-Am, and things started to get much more intense. More Europeans showed up, and riders like Pierre Karsmakers and Mick Andrews joined Joel Robert and Gunnar Lindstrom. America put up the best we had, including flat-track champion Dick Mann, Dave Aldana, John DeSoto, and a few others, with me included. Basically, we got our butts kicked; however, we were learning fast. And, for me, it was fun. We got to travel and watch the fans go wild. The sport was catching on and I was lucky enough to be a part.

I think that within a year, motocross racing in California was roaring. We started racing at many tracks, including Hopetown, Westlake Village, Carlsbad, Bay Mare, Saddleback, Lake Elsinore, and Castaic. The bikes were changing as fast as the tracks were developing. The big four [motorcycle manufacturers] from Japan hit the United States, and there would be no turning back for them.

As for my experience, I started racing motocross with a Hodoka Ace, then a Greeves, a Sachs, and a Penton. Next I switched to a Bultaco, then Kawasaki, and finally Honda. Although I continued racing motocross until 1974, I believe '69 was a turning point in my life. I was the first American to beat the European riders. It was July 4, 1969, at Saddleback Park in Southern California, something I remain very proud of in my career. My brother and I actually promoted a motocross race in an enclosed track at Ascot Park Raceway in Southern California late in 1969 and I started my motocross school that same year. The school would end up taking me further than my racing career could have ever done.

By the 1970s, America began to produce a home-grown crop of motocross riders who were young, fearless, and undaunted by the European threat. Names like Jimmy Weinert, Brad Lackey, Tony DiStefano, Jim Pomeroy, Mark Blackwell, Gary Semics, Barry Higgins, and Sonny DeFeo began making headlines. The Inter-Am series became the Trans-AMA series with AMA sanctioning. America was on its way to becoming a motocross battleground. (For a more in-depth look at the history of motocross in America, see *Motocross America* by Bill Amick.)

Unknown to those who were busy launching motocross in the United States, events were taking place simultaneously in Southern California that would propel the fledgling sport into its second generation. Far removed from any headline or magazine article, a young boy began to explore the joys of riding a tiny, hand-built motorcycle over the vast wilderness called the Mojave Desert.

It was a time before mega-millions of people crammed themselves into California and caused the wilderness to give way to freeways, bad air, and houses packed side-by-side to the horizon. The desert was still a challenge to those who came, but it also offered freedom. For those brave enough to ignore the sand, rocks, snakes, insects, and pucker bushes, rugged trails rewarded challengers with unlimited space and a chance to test their abilities against nature. It is little wonder why the desert became so popular with those who loved motorcycles.

One of the big names in motocross during the late 1970s was the great "Tony D," Tony DiStefano, riding for Suzuki. Tony won the 250cc Outdoor National Championship in 1975, 1976, and 1977. In 1975 and 1976, he won with none other than Keith McCarty as his mechanic. *Steve Reyes*

Hannah raced the European riders on on their turf, too, but did better against them in America. He is shown here in Gaildorf, Germany, at the 1978 Motocross des Nations race. The American team did not win the 1978 title, but Bob did beat the Europeans overall by winning the 1978 Trans-AMA U.S.A. series. *Moto Verte; Terry Good*

As for the young boy on the handmade motorcycle, he was born in the desert. He learned its secrets and its dangers. He loved the desert, and it understood. The desert never hurt the boy or caused him worry. The desert became the boy's mentor and released all its wisdom. When the boy became a man, the lessons learned from the desert would serve him well.

Until the day he retired, Hurricane Bob Hannah could ride with the best in the world. Bob remarked, “The only thing that slowed me down was the injuries, from the time I broke my leg until I retired. It was a struggle to rehab, get back into riding shape, and then compete against the new crop of young riders. Every guy coming up wanted a piece of me.” *TMP*

2

MINIBIKES, BUNNY HOPPING, AND NEVER EATING DIRT

Getting Bob Hannah to recount his accomplishments on a motorcycle can be difficult. But when I asked about riding in the desert with his Dad and Uncle Mel, saving money for his first Husqvarna, or getting his full factory ride with Yamaha, he fired right up and talked about how he began the process of leaving his indelible mark on the art of riding a motorcycle.

BOB HANNAH

I was born in Lancaster, California, but we actually lived in a town called Quartz Hills. At the time, none of that area had been developed, so most of the desert was still wide open and free. My dad, Wild Bill, worked day shift at Lockheed Aircraft in Palmdale. As far back as I can remember, my mom, Barbara, took care of the house and my sister, Tammy, who is five years younger than me.

My dad was always a hardcore desert rider, as was my uncle Mel. In fact, my uncle Mel was an outstanding hillclimb rider and was the first ever to clear the Matterhorn at Saddleback Park. When they built the hillclimb at Saddleback, nobody could climb it until my uncle showed up. He did it, no problem. Both my dad and uncle were great hillclimb riders. I can't remember a time when my dad didn't have a motorcycle.

Above: Wild Bill Hannah, shown here on his 650cc Triumph in the mid-1950s, not only taught the Hurricane to ride but built him his first bike. The Hurricane's dad rode in the desert or on the street nearly every day of his life. *Bob Hannah*

Left: This very rare photo shows Uncle Mel exercising his hillclimbing skills back when helmets were not required. Uncle Mel was a true pioneer and was the first to climb the Matterhorn at Saddleback Park. *Bob Hannah*

When I was about seven years old, my dad took a Honda 55 and built a minibike for me. Back then, they didn't have production minibikes. So he took the Honda, lowered it, put on a bicycle seat and a gas tank from a moped, and I had a dirt mini.

From that day on I was riding. I could ride out of my backyard into the desert without any restrictions. As soon as I got comfortable, I started riding with my dad. Nearly every day, when I got home from school and he came home from work, we would spend a couple hours riding. Both my dad and uncle were way ahead of their time in developing a riding style for the dirt. I started copying everything my dad did on his bike. Hillclimbing, jumping ruts, bank jumping, reading terrain. I didn't know at the time how important all this would be. I just wanted to be like my dad.

I fell into a pattern. If I wasn't riding my minibike I was riding a bicycle with the kids in the neighborhood. On weekends, my dad and I would hit the road, either going out riding in the desert with Uncle Mel, or, if it was the season, we would go hunting and fishing. I was an outdoor kid. I was getting an education that would help me for the rest of my career and life. From as far back as I can remember, I loved the wilderness. And the more I learned about it, the more comfortable I felt.

Like all kids, I wanted to do things better than everyone I hung out with. I guess I was a little on the wild side, and when we all started to do jumps and tricks on our bikes, it was my signal to do something wilder and more daring than the rest of my friends.

Before long, we were serious about outdoing each other, and we started having contests to see who was the most daring. I got pretty good and began experimenting with jumps. I started jumping curbs and then it was a fifty-five-gallon drum lying on its side. I invented what we called "hop jumping," or "bunny hopping." After I developed the hop jump to the point where I could out-jump the other kids, I took it one step further. By today's standards it would be considered a really dumb idea, but I got ten kids to lie on the ground side by side and I jumped them without using a ramp. Nobody wanted to challenge that trick and I became champ of the local bicycle tricks.

For a while I raced bicycle motocross. I even started winning, and I liked the feeling, but after about twenty-five or thirty races, I just faded out of the picture, no real reason. I was spending more time riding in the desert. After the minibike my dad built, I got a Hodaka 90 and after about a year moved up to a Hodaka 100. After that my dad bought me a Yamaha MX125.

During my middle school and high school years, I became kind of a loner. I was not too interested in school activities—with the exception of being part of the wrestling team during the winter months. But, as soon as the weather turned good, I was gone. In fact, except for my time bicycle racing, most of the people I hung out with were older guys, friends of my dad and uncle who rode the desert.

As time went on I began to teach myself how to ride faster and faster. My dad had warned me when I first started not to fall off and wreck the bike. He would tell me that if I fell, I could get hurt—or worse, crash the bike and not be able to fix it. So I learned to stay on no matter what happened. I can count the times I fell in those early days on one hand.

Right: Bob Hannah, his sister, Tammy ("Red"), and his dad, Wild Bill, in 1986 at Lake Isabella, California. Wild Bill taught Bob to ride at a very young age, but, more importantly, he taught him not to fall off. *Hannah*

An example of how to check front tire wear without stopping. Hannah admitted many times he was not the most stylish rider, but his dad taught him to stay with the motorcycle no matter what happened. Hannah would always say, "If you fall off, you can't win." *Werner Straub; Terry Good*

As a consequence of my not wanting to crash, I began to learn how to use the bike, the suspension and brakes. I began to develop a style, a rhythm; it was like music. I would ride, and the faster I rode, the more tempo and harmony controlled my actions. It was like the bike was a part of my being and everything just flowed. I would ride alone in the middle of nowhere for hours on end, and slowly a style developed that could be considered all mine.

This idea of not falling carried over throughout my career. I would never give up in a crash. I never just jumped off. I fought all the way. People would wonder why I just didn't fall. The reasoning was that if you fall you can't win and winning was everything—but more about that later.

As time went by, I deliberately started testing myself more and more. I jumped ditches, climbed banks, and rode hills flat out over the roughest terrain in the desert. The kids who rode the desert, myself included, began inventing riding styles that had never been seen. When you ride every day, you find yourself looking at the wildest conditions as normal. If we took a really good motocross rider out in the desert with us, we would make fools of them. We invented radical riding, only nobody ever saw what we were doing so it stayed out in the desert.

Most people think that I sort of grew into motocross racing over a long period of time. Not true! It happened in one day in July 1974. I had never been to a motorcycle motocross race in my life. The truth of the matter is that a friend of mine named Mick McKee, who was a riding buddy of my dad, was the one who got the whole thing started. Mick was about fifty-five years old and had been riding the desert for years. We would talk about racing all the time, but nothing ever came of the conversations.

Finally, when I graduated from high school in 1974, he asked me if I wanted to ride his CZ at Indian Dunes Motorcycle Park. Up to that point my dad never wanted me to race. But when I got out of high school, I moved out on my own and then figured I could do what I wanted. We went to the track and I was given some basic instructions on what was going to happen. They stuck me in an intermediate class and so I lined up and waited for the gate to drop. I won my first race that day and thought it was a pretty cool experience. So, the following week McKee asked if I wanted to ride in the expert class. It was a challenge and I took it as such. I figured that McKee was trying to test me to see if I would chicken out. I wasn't about to do that. I think I finished fourth. McKee was impressed and suggested that I run a few more races, but I would have to move from Quartz Hills to Los Angeles so it would be easier to get to the tracks. McKee said, "Come down to L.A. and get a job and we'll go race a few events."

Although I didn't like the city, Los Angeles was not something totally new. I had spent about a year living in Whittier, so I knew a little about the area. Still, coming from the desert into the smog and traffic made me feel a little tense. I landed a job welding exhaust pipes at a place called J&R Expansion Chambers. Once I got settled, I raced McKee's CZ for twelve weekends straight. We ran Indian Dunes, Saddleback, Carlsbad, Valley Cycle Park, Escape Country—all of the local tracks. It didn't take long before we realized that I needed more bike. McKee had the CZ running as good as it could, but we still couldn't stay with the fast guys. There was no way I wanted to get dusted week after week by guys I could outride just because they had faster bikes.

I made a decision, the first in my series of pivotal points that will appear throughout my career. I quit racing for a short time and saved every penny I made with the intention of buying my own race bike. I set a budget of fifteen dollars a week for rent and fifteen dollars a week for food, not one cent more. Everything after thirty dollars went toward the price of the bike.

continued on page 34

TAMMY HANNAH DORY

Everyone who was part of the Hannah inner circle of friends loved Ashley the Wonder Dog. Bob once left her with the author and his wife while he flew out of town on business. After Ashley understood that Bob had gone without her, she refused to let anyone pet her and just lay in the corner until his return. *TMP*

Bob's sister, Tammy, has been one of his biggest fans since the very beginning of his career. About her relationship with Bob, Tammy says, "Growing up I couldn't have had a better role model." *Hannah*

THERE ARE FEW WHO KNOW the Hurricane down to the core of his spirit. One person who does is his younger sister, Tammy. Known to everyone in the motocross racing business as "Red" because of her red hair, Tammy has always thought of Bob Hannah not just as a champion racer, but as her big brother and sometime father figure. Here's what it's like to be sister to a hurricane.

Now married, Tammy Dory is still "Red" to everyone in the motocross racing business. Tammy has taken up flying and she and her husband, Joe, restore and repair airplanes for a living. *Hannah*

TAMMY

When my brother graduated from high school, my mom and dad separated. My mother and I moved to Canada and Bob started racing. He moved from our home in Quartz Hills to Whittier, California, got a job welding exhaust pipes, and bought a race bike.

Once Bob went professional and began getting paid, he would send me airplane tickets so I could be with him at the races. So I was able to witness his rise from wild kid riding in the desert to champion. It was a very exciting time.

Although Bob was still young, barely an adult, he cared about his family first and foremost. While my mom and I lived in Canada, Bob helped support us and made sure we were comfortable. In fact, even before we moved, Bob would always take care of me; he would give me an allowance when I was a little kid, taking money from what he would earn mowing lawns or fixing bicycles.

In 1979, I returned to the United States and lived with Bob at his home in Carson City, Nevada. He had a duplex, so I had my own world and I was able to finish high school. When Bob moved to Ketchum, Idaho, of course I tagged along. His first house in Ketchum was very close to the home once lived in by Ernest Hemingway. It was a great feeling to do my morning workout and run past such a wonderful piece of history.

I need to regress back to my earlier days before proceeding. From the time I was a little girl, Bob has always looked after me. Older kids hate the idea of having to deal with a younger sibling, but Bob enjoyed the idea. Taking care of me was part of Bob's personality. He has always been willing to give or share with others he has affection for.

The second part of his make-up is his drive. My mother would tell me about his drive and how, at the age of four, he would collect pop bottles and turn them in for the deposits. He put every penny in the bank. As he got older, he did all kinds of odd jobs, always saving part of the money and sharing the rest. When he was sixteen be bought a pickup truck—cash, no help from anyone. So, to me, there is nothing unusual about the fact that when Bob went from dirt poor to winning championships and having a factory ride, his very first priority was to take care of his mom and his sister.

Now gone, Ashley the Wonder Dog belonged to everyone. If you hung out with Hannah, you had Ashley as your dog. *TMP*

Money is very important to Bob. It allows him to live his life on his terms. But winning is his number one objective when it comes to competition. Bob has told me many times winning was everything and second place was nothing.

Although he has tremendous ability, uncanny balance, and has been riding motorcycles since he was a toddler, Bob has always had to train hard, practice endlessly, and work diligently to stay ahead. He underrates his awesome talent. Bob will tell you that riders like Jeremy McGrath, James Stewart, David Bailey, and Ricky Carmichael have great style. Bob contends his style was staying on the bike no matter what and he had to work harder than anyone just to be able to win.

As a reminder of Ashley the Wonder Dog, Bob's ranch and business carry a tribute to how much Ashley meant to everyone who ever gave her a pat on the head. *TMP*

Growing up, I couldn't have had a better role model. Bob never let me dwell on the negative side of life. I remember when he broke his leg. I was there when the doctors wanted to amputate his leg because of an infection. He didn't allow it. That would be negative, and he knew he could overcome the problem. When he started his rehab training, he proved his point, and by the time he was ready to ride, I think he was better and faster than he had ever been.

I learned that you never tell Bob Hannah he can't do something. I knew that every time he was hurt he would come back stronger. Watching him made me stronger.

My favorite story about his determination came about when he was picked for the U.S. Motocross des Nations team. He was with Suzuki, and it was late in his career. Right away the rumors starting flying—Hannah is too old; don't pick Hannah, he's washed up.

He proved them all wrong.

There is no way that I will ever be able to pay back my brother for all he has done for me, but I do take comfort in the fact that I was the one who brought Ashley the Wonder Dog into his life. I got Ashley as a puppy, but the moment she saw Bob, she left me and went to him. After that the two of them were inseparable. Ashley became his hunting partner, his co-pilot, and part of his inner circle. All of us who were close to Bob loved Ashley.

In the end, Bob was the single most influential person of my life and I can't imagine life without him.

continued from page 30

I was living in a house in Orange County with four other guys with not much in the way of luxury accommodations. Lucky for me, the house was located in a rural area with an avocado orchard next door. So, when I ran out of money for food I would go into the orchard at night and pick avocados off the ground, put them in brown paper bags, and place the bags on windowsills around the house so they could get ripe. I would live on avocado sandwiches. To this day I love avocado/chicken sandwiches, and every time I have one I think of those days.

In January of 1975, I bought a new 250cc Husqvarna from Steve Herd's bike shop in Whittier. I paid cash: ones, fives, tens, change; all of my savings. Now I had a fast bike and no money. McKee acted as my mechanic and hauled me to the races. I started winning a few events and began butting heads with riders like Rex Staten, John DeSoto, guys you read about in the magazines. My first lesson was that these guys were tough and fast. They didn't give you anything. If you wanted to win, you had to ride your ass off or stay home.

Mick McKee and I worked together for a time, but the bike wasn't his and he sort of lost interest in just hanging out, so I began doing all of the mechanical work and race preparation myself.

Working for a living limited the amount of time I could devote to race preparation. I was making about $150 for a forty-hour week. I had to work nights on the bike and hustle to the track early Saturday, ride all day, clean the bike, fix what was broken, and then race on Sunday. By Monday morning I was beat.

Then I started to win prize money and that changed things in a hurry. One weekend I made $300 and realized that I could make a living racing motorcycles.

This photo of Bob Hannah in his days as a privateer racer displays the riding style soon to become his trademark. Bob used everything he had to pay for this bike, a Husky, then earned enough money running it at local events to allow him to continue until he was discovered. *Bob Hannah*

Early in his fantastic career, a young, blond Bob Hannah (far right) was named to the 1978 United States Motocross des Nations team. The other members included (from left to right) Chuck Sun, Tommy Croft, and Rick Burgett. *Moto Verte; Terry Good*

The only obstacle for me was my lack of consistency. One week I would win, the next week run seventh. So, I was forced to keep my job.

There was one way to cure the problem. I trained harder and rode harder than I had ever done and finally, on July 8, 1975, one year after I started working at the welding shop, I quit and went racing on my own full-time. The second of my pivotal points had been reached.

Once on my own, paying the bills and making money became paramount in my life. I was riding my Husky and doing a reasonable job, but being a one-man band wasn't the best idea going. Then I got a break. A fellow named Gary Harlow, who owned a company called DG Performance Specialties in Anaheim, California, called me and he wanted me to ride for him. Harlow was a pioneer in the motocross accessory business and his company sold everything for the racer, from chest protectors to boots, shirts, helmets, tote bags, and pipes. He also worked with most of the bike manufacturers and had a full line of bikes in his shop at all times. Our deal would be him paying me a few bucks a month for expenses, and he would furnish me a van and a mechanic for all the races we ran. I accepted and started riding anything and everything: 125cc to 250cc, Yamaha, Honda, Husky, and Suzuki.

While riding for Harlow, or it could have been just prior to me signing with him, Suzuki asked if I could ride a couple weekends for them. I did, and finished behind Marty Smith and Tommy Croft. So, after those two weekends, Suzuki told me that they didn't have a program set up, but if I would stay in touch, they were interested in me riding their bikes. I stayed in touch and, finally, Suzuki told me they were bringing new bikes to America and asked if I wanted to ride. I said okay, but never really thought they would call again. I figured they were blowing smoke up my butt, so I concentrated on riding for Gary Harlow. A couple of months later, Suzuki called, told me the bikes were in and, if I wanted to ride, to get over to the headquarters right away. I talked to the Suzuki race manager named Tosh Koyama and he agreed that I would ride the new 125cc, 250cc, and 500cc bikes in local events. In the first three months, I rode a bunch of races and won all but a couple. I remember having mechanical failures, or I would have won every race I ran.

We ran all of the big money races in the CMC [Continental Motosport Club] schedule that were available, and it ended up being a really good deal for me. Suddenly, I was making a couple grand a month and, in 1975, that was a good payday.

On top of my prize money, Suzuki was paying me $800 a month plus expenses. I had a company van, but no mechanic. I had to do all my own preparation and maintenance. I changed tires, shocks, whatever needed to be done between motos. So, instead of sitting on my ass drinking iced tea between motos like the riders with factory mechanics, I had to work my brains out. Thank God for all that time in the desert. I was used to riding all day and working on my own bike.

Making money riding a motorcycle had its appeal, and I liked the idea of racing for a living. However, there was a rather large group of riders who would just as soon have me disappear than to contend with another guy trying to take away their living. Racing for money was way different than racing for fun. Handlebar-to-handlebar racing was tough business—especially when you threw in a few punches, rams, kicks, and guys who would run you over to win.

I had a very hard lesson on my first outing away from California. While I was riding for Gary Harlow, we took an excursion to a couple of 125 Nationals—one in Texas and the other in New Orleans. Well, the hot, humid weather in New Orleans and my fondness for air conditioning caused me to fall victim to heat exhaustion. I didn't drink enough water, I was not in the best shape, and the result was riders laughing their collective asses off at me and a trip in an ambulance after I passed out. I swore that would be the last time anyone ever laughed at me. My answer was to begin a serious training program. I got a book written by World Champion Rolf Tibblen and followed the instructions faithfully. I started running, lifting weights, and managing my diet. The more I trained, the better I got, and the faster I could ride. The rougher the track, the more comfortable I felt.

My attitude began to change along with the improvements in my riding style. I started considering other riders the enemy. I had some friends, but that was off the track. When the starting gate dropped, I wanted to beat every rider there. They all stood between me and a payday. I was riding for a living and it was win or starve and I wasn't about to keep living on avocado sandwiches.

As time went by, the local races allowed me to work on my style and learn how to actually race. Because of the years of desert riding, I had perfected the art of using a front brake. That is the biggest factor in getting into and out of corners. At the time, a lot of the riders didn't know how to use their front brakes and that gave me a slight advantage. Second, my training started to show signs of results. In truth, I was using local races as stepping stones to something bigger; the only problem was I didn't know what was coming next. In the mid-1970s, riding the Nationals was the place to make real money. Some of the Europeans like Pierre Karsmakers were getting $75,000 a year. I wanted a piece of that action. But Suzuki management didn't think I could win at the Nationals and to be honest there were doubts in my mind as well.

Then, without much warning, another one of those pivotal points in my career that seemed to control my destiny appeared out of nowhere.

My friend Gary Harlow called me and said, "Hey, Yamaha would like to talk to you about riding their bikes. Do you want to talk to them?" Because I had ridden for Gary, trusted him, and knew that he was really on top of things in the motorcycle business, it was easy to make a decision. Besides, Harlow had been promoting Yamaha

Left and opposite page: When Hannah went back to Suzuki at the end of his career, the idea was for him to conduct bike development and public relations and not race full time. Here he is "developing" the bike at a Supercross race at the Los Angeles Coliseum in 1986. Racing was a great way to see how well new parts could perform. It was also a good way for the Hurricane to stay connected to his fans. *TMP*

and the factory respected his judgment, so if he thought talking to me was a good idea, then the management would go along. Looking back, Gary Harlow played a major role in those first talks with Yamaha.

My career was only one year and three months old and I was as naïve as anyone could be. I really didn't know many people, didn't know the ropes when it came to contracts or becoming a professional.

At this point I didn't even have a car. I had a Suzuki van, but I could only use it on weekends to go to the races. They had given me a 50cc motorbike to ride during the week. So Gary had to pick me up and we headed over to Yamaha.

Harlow gave me much-needed support and he had promoted me to Yamaha before my meeting, so they were ready to talk when I arrived. The meeting was with a man named Pete Schick, manager of the race team, and Mel Callaway, the president of Yamaha USA.

They asked if I wanted to ride the Nationals for the 1976 season. This was November of 1975 and they wanted me to be ready for the summer of '76. The deal was a full factory ride, works bike, mechanic, van, expenses, and $1000 a month salary. I told them, "I'll get back to you."

The next day, I went to Suzuki and met with T. Shiganoya and told him that I wanted to ride the Nationals with a full factory ride. I also told him that Yamaha had offered me a full-time ride. He said, "Yamaha offered you a ride? I don't believe you."

Then he asked me, "Can you beat our factory riders?" I told him no, not yet, but soon. Then he said, "I want you to ride local for a couple more years". "No," I said to him, "I don't want to do that."

The meeting was put on hold and I was told to sit in a waiting area. About two hours later the president of Suzuki came out and said he called Yamaha and they told him that there was no contract offer for a factory ride. I shot back that I didn't know what to tell them, but the offer had been made. I was dismissed.

The next day I called Gary Harlow and told him, "Let's go to Yamaha and sign the deal."

It was a Wednesday and I signed the deal. On Thursday, I went to Suzuki to work on my bikes for the upcoming weekend race. It was my regular schedule. Every Thursday I loaded up two bikes, a 250cc and a 370cc, to go the desert to practice ride with my dad on Friday. Then I would go to the biggest money race of the weekend and race Saturday and Sunday. So, as I'm loading the bikes, one of the Japanese guys came out of the building and asked, "Did you sign with Yamaha?" I said yes. He told me, "Leave everything and get out!" The guy was so pissed I couldn't believe it. He kept yelling, "Take your personal shit and leave everything that belongs to Suzuki right where it is." Then he had a couple of security guards take me off the property. I had to call a buddy to get a ride home.

I called Yamaha and told them that I got fired and I wanted to race a money event at Valley Cycle Park. I needed the money and, by this time, I was so pissed at Suzuki I didn't care what happened. Yamaha said, "What classes do you want to race?" I told them 125cc and 250cc. Yamaha said, "Go to the track. We'll have two factory bikes, a mechanic, a van, and everything you need." I won both classes and the team from Suzuki went nuts. They were so pissed, and I just sat back and laughed.

A young Bob Hannah riding at the peak of his career put Yamaha into the spotlight as a winning manufacturer. In 1979 the Hurricane was the most feared rider in America. Shortly after he clinched the 1979 250 National Championship, his career nearly came to an end because of a water-skiing accident. *Yamaha PR; Dennis Kanegae*

3

WEATHER ALERT: HURRICANE GATHERING ON THE HORIZON

Dennis Kanegae, a longtime friend of Bob Hannah, was an employee at Yamaha during the early days of the factory's relationship with the Hurricane. In 1975, Kanegae had given up a career as a flat-track racer to become a factory test rider for Yamaha. Dennis offered to share his memories of those early days and his friendship with Bob Hannah.

DENNIS KANEGAE

At the time Hannah came into my world, I was working at Yamaha as a test rider for both production bikes and for prototype engineering projects. The department I worked in was under the factory racing program and the manager was a fellow named Pete Schick.

One day Pete calls me into his office and asks me to do him a favor. He was looking at a young kid who was riding local events and he wanted me to take him riding and do some personal evaluation. He said something to the effect of "Take this kid out to Saddleback and see what he can do." It was a little out of my normal duties, but anytime I could get out of the office and go riding it was a great day. I met Bob and said, "Hi, my name is Dennis and I'm going to take you riding. I don't know exactly why, but let's just go."

We loaded up a couple of YZ250 bikes and headed for Saddleback. About ten minutes after we unloaded and started getting warmed up, Bob started jumping cliffs, ditches, and jumping over my head as I'm riding down a trail. He was doing things on a motorcycle that I had never seen before. He was inventing freestyle riding right in front of my eyes.

Basically, he was defying gravity. We rode for about an hour or so and I was just blown away by his talent, fearless riding style, and control. I couldn't believe that anyone could ride like he did.

Wild Bill in his senior years still rode the dirt of the California desert. This author rode with Bill when the man was nearly 80 years old, and I was humbled by his skill and daring. *Bob Hannah*

We headed back to our van and, when we got there, parked about a hundred feet away was an old El Camino and two grizzly old guys unloading a couple of custom-built hillclimb specials. They were Triumph frames with custom engines and a long-wheelbase design, strictly built for climbing. At the time, Saddleback had this hill called the Matterhorn and it was brutal. The last forty feet to the top was nearly vertical. These guys were getting ready to attempt to climb the Matterhorn.

Now Bob's uncle Mel was a hillclimb champion back in the day, and he was the first rider to top the Matterhorn. So, we started talking to these guys and they started telling us stories about hillclimbing and how they knew all about Mel Hannah.

After a few more stories, Bob said, "Hey, I'm about ready to take off and head home." I said, "Okay let's pack up." Then, without warning, Bob jumped on one of the YZs and headed for the Matterhorn. Everybody froze. Before anyone could take a deep breath, Hannah went straight up the Matterhorn on a stock Yamaha YZ250. The two hillclimbers were speechless and their eyes were popping out of their heads. They couldn't believe what they just saw. We could hear Bob on the top of the Matterhorn spinning donuts and playing around. Then I told the two old guys, "You ain't seen anything yet."

Opposite: What's wrong with this picture? The Hurricane is showing off his style, not on his factory works 250cc Yamaha, but on a YZ-80 during a 1978 film shoot for the Yamaha public relations department. *Dennis Kanegae*

Suddenly, Bob jumped off the top of the Matterhorn and rode straight down. To my knowledge, that had never been done before.

I started telling the two old timers that this kid lived in the desert and his dad taught him to ride and he had been riding since he was seven years old. They didn't even hear me, they just kept staring.

That was my introduction to Bob Hannah.

I went back to Yamaha and told them, "Yes, Hannah might become a good racer, but it is his ability to handle a bike in nonracing circumstances that is impressive. Those years of riding alone over some of the most rugged terrain you can think up have made him capable of handling a bike under any condition." I told Pete Schick, "You think Kenny Roberts is good, Hannah does things on a bike I have never seen done before."

In the winter of 1975, Hannah went down to the Florida series and just decimated the field. He kicked ass. It was very evident that here was a guy to be reckoned with.

In 1976 I was transferred from the testing department at Yamaha to the public relations department, and part of my new job was to deal with the press and set up opportunities for our riders to get exposure. During the 1976 125cc Nationals, Hannah started winning. At the time, Marty Smith was America's motocross hero. Honda had a strong team and were dominating the AMA National series in 125cc. Then here comes Hannah, kicking the hero's butt. Honda didn't like it, Marty didn't like it, and some of the press didn't like it, either.

Bob was not the type of personality like a Roger DeCoster, Tony DiStefano, or Jimmy Weinert. DeCoster was a superstar. Marty Smith was good-looking; he was from San Diego and had a surfer image, and the press loved him. Bob was a bashful kid from the desert who started out with nothing and was earning his way. He was shy with people, especially the press, and journalists interpreted his manner as being a snob. Also, Bob is very truthful, and it seemed that every time he opened his mouth he would cause some type of controversy. If someone attacked him, he would attack back. Sometimes that is not the best way to get good press. Most of the time it was hard for Hannah to show his real feelings; consequently he built up a shield to protect himself. Under all the smoke he was just a nice kid from the desert.

In his first year as a factory rider, Bob Hannah fought a season-long war with then reigning two-time 125cc Outdoor National Champion Marty Smith. Marty (shown here) was considered a hero to race fans, and they were not thrilled to have a wild kid from the desert take the title. *Steve Reyes*

The 1976 AMA Outdoor National Motocross Championship for the 125cc class was a turning point in Bob Hannah's career. He was now a factory rider, properly moving on from his local notoriety as an up-and-coming rider. He was a professional, with all of the attendant benefits—and responsibilities. In telling the story of that pivotal year, we shall rely on two additional sources for an accurate account of what happened.

Bill Buchka was Bob Hannah's Yamaha factory-appointed mechanic for the 1976 season, and Terry Good was another rider. In fact, after a long tape recording session about that fateful season, Hannah admitted that his memory of the details during 1976 were at best uncertain. He said, "Hey, it's been thirty-two years and I can't remember all the details." It was then Hannah himself suggested I call Terry and Bill. I did and discovered they had indeed preserved the story far better than Bob. Together, the two put together a very concise, detailed story of each race that led, ultimately, to the first AMA pro championship for Bob Hannah.

To best appreciate the climatic results of the battle to capture the 1976 125cc National Championship,

The press reporters didn't realize that Hannah was all about winning. He simply wanted to win more than anyone he was racing. To Bob, second place was worthless.

In the end, the press had to deal with Bob because he became a superstar. But to this day I think that Bob never felt comfortable doing interviews, but it was something that he learned to live with and accept as part of the job.

I tried to smooth over the lumps between Hannah and the press. In one case, *Motocross Action* magazine was very hard on Bob. They would constantly rake him over the coals. So, in order to try and improve relations and to get some understanding about Hannah, I set up a dinner meeting in Atlanta before one of the Nationals and invited Bob and a *Motocross Action* staffer. My mistake was to have the dinner at a sushi bar. I'm Japanese, so I figured everybody loved sushi. Hannah was from the desert. He had never even seen sushi; hamburgers and fries were his idea of dinner. When he came in and realized raw fish was the highlight of the meal, he said, "What the f**k is this?" It was pretty funny.

Another of the early stars of American motocross was Jimmy Ellis, riding for Can-Am. Ellis was tough, fast, and willing to give 100 percent every time. *Steve Reyes*

a certain degree of scene setting and background revelation must take place. An epic confrontation was about to occur, and there would be casualties and battles lost. A king would be dethroned, egos would be crushed, and feelings would be battered. An outsider would challenge the establishment. It would all play out like a dark comedy from the pen of William Shakespeare, had he only been lucky enough to live in an age of dirt bikes.

At the time, Honda had established its name in American motocross racing, and Honda rider Marty Smith was considered by many to be unbeatable in the 125cc class. So the plan Honda envisioned for 1976 was to expand on this advantage by Smith both winning a third straight 125cc championship title in the United States and attempting a world championship title challenge as a bonus. Honda was promoting their highly successful Elsinore models and, by using Smith's winning record, good looks, and movie star image, they were increasing sales in the American market. It was a prosperous formula, and Honda did not want their plan altered in any way.

One of the riders Hannah looked up to when he began his career was Steve Stackable on his Maico. *Steve Reyes*

Yamaha, on the other hand, was ready to introduce their newest creation. It was called the OW, and it featured a water-cooled YZ125 engine with much improved horsepower readings and, more important, a monoshock rear suspension that would forever change the paradigm of off-road and road-going motorcycle design.

The 1976 season would involve all the major manufacturers and a field of extremely talented and aggressive riders. Honda had all their eggs in the Marty Smith basket. Kawasaki was pinning their hopes on Steve Wise. Husqvarna had Swedish standout Nils Arne Nilsson. Can-Am would field Jimmy Ellis to ride their new water-cooled 125; Ellis was a tough, fearless rider who had put on a spectacular show while winning the Super Bowl of Motocross at the Los Angeles Coliseum in 1975. Suzuki teamed Billy Grossi and Danny LaPorte for the start of the season, and would add Jeff Jennings later. Yamaha hired Danny Turner, a privateer who had been outstanding in the 1975 AMA Outdoor National season, and a wild young teen from the desert town of Quartz Hills, California, named Bob Hannah.

The 1976 125cc National Championship series would feature eight races, beginning in April at Hangtown in California and ending in August in New Orleans. Without question, Marty Smith was considered a favorite, expected to win a third straight title. But there was a change in the Honda camp for 1976: Smith would have a new mechanic, a young man named Dave Arnold. Despite his lack of experience, Arnold had been hired by Honda as a general mechanic, and for him to be assigned to the national champion was a daunting task.

There were some changes for Hannah as well—ironically, the exact reverse of the Smith situation at Honda. Hannah's 1975 mechanic, Don Dudek, had been replaced by Bill Buchka. But, unlike Dave Arnold, Buchka was a seasoned veteran who had worked with champion riders like Pierre Karsmakers. So, while Honda had a rookie mechanic working with a veteran rider, Yamaha put a veteran mechanic with a rookie rider. Buchka admitted he was worried about working with a rookie, but had been impressed with Hannah's riding ability the few time he had seen him race.

Oh no! Hannah flies through the air with his hand raised in victory, thinking he has just passed for the lead. In reality he has merely passed Jim Pomeroy for second place and still has a long way to go. *Larry Maiers*

BOB HANNAH

The 1976 season was the start of what I called my short-lived career. I truly believed I would sign for one year and, at the end of that year, I would be out of work and back driving heavy equipment or welding expansion chambers. I figured I had fooled them, and I would have one year as a professional.

I looked at what I had in front of me and thought, "Hey, this is a great deal and I better enjoy it while I can." I had a full factory ride paying a grand a month, my own mechanic, a van, travel expenses, and a bonus program for winning races or if I won a series championship.

The 1976 season began with the Florida series; a five-race training series is what I called it. Although I had been hired to ride the Nationals on a 125, Yamaha wanted me to ride a 500 in the Florida series. I was teamed with Rick Burgett at the time, and we were both riding Yamaha OW26 500s.

Opposite: When Hannah was at the peak of his career, he worked out in his gym at home in Idaho every chance he could. His incentive to overcome any challenge was stimulated by a life-size photo of Roger DeCoster by his punching bag. *TMP*

As it worked out, I won the 500cc class in the series. I remember having some knockout battles with Steve Stackable, who was the hot shoe at the time. But, the big thing about that series was the fact that I started learning just how professional motocross racing worked. It was the first time I had been on the road for a long period of time, and it took me a while to get adjusted. But the bottom line was that I could win, and I took that attitude into the Nationals.

As I said, I thought I would last a year, and then be back working a regular job. But after the Florida series, I began to realize that if I put in the work and trained hard, practiced hard, I could win. My attitude changed and I began to gain confidence.

One thing was for sure—I had learned my lesson in 1975 when I got heat exhaustion in New Orleans and passed out and ended up in the hospital. I would never use air-conditioning in a hotel or rental car; I lived in the elements, no matter how tough. I trained in every type of weather condition throughout the entire '76 season. I was never going to get laughed at again. Never!

A teammate of the Hurricane in the early days of Team Yamaha was super-fast Rick "The Lumberjack" Burgett. Burgett won the AMA 500cc Outdoor National Championship in 1978, while the Hurricane took the 250cc Outdoor National, Supercross, and Trans-AMA titles. *Steve Reyes*

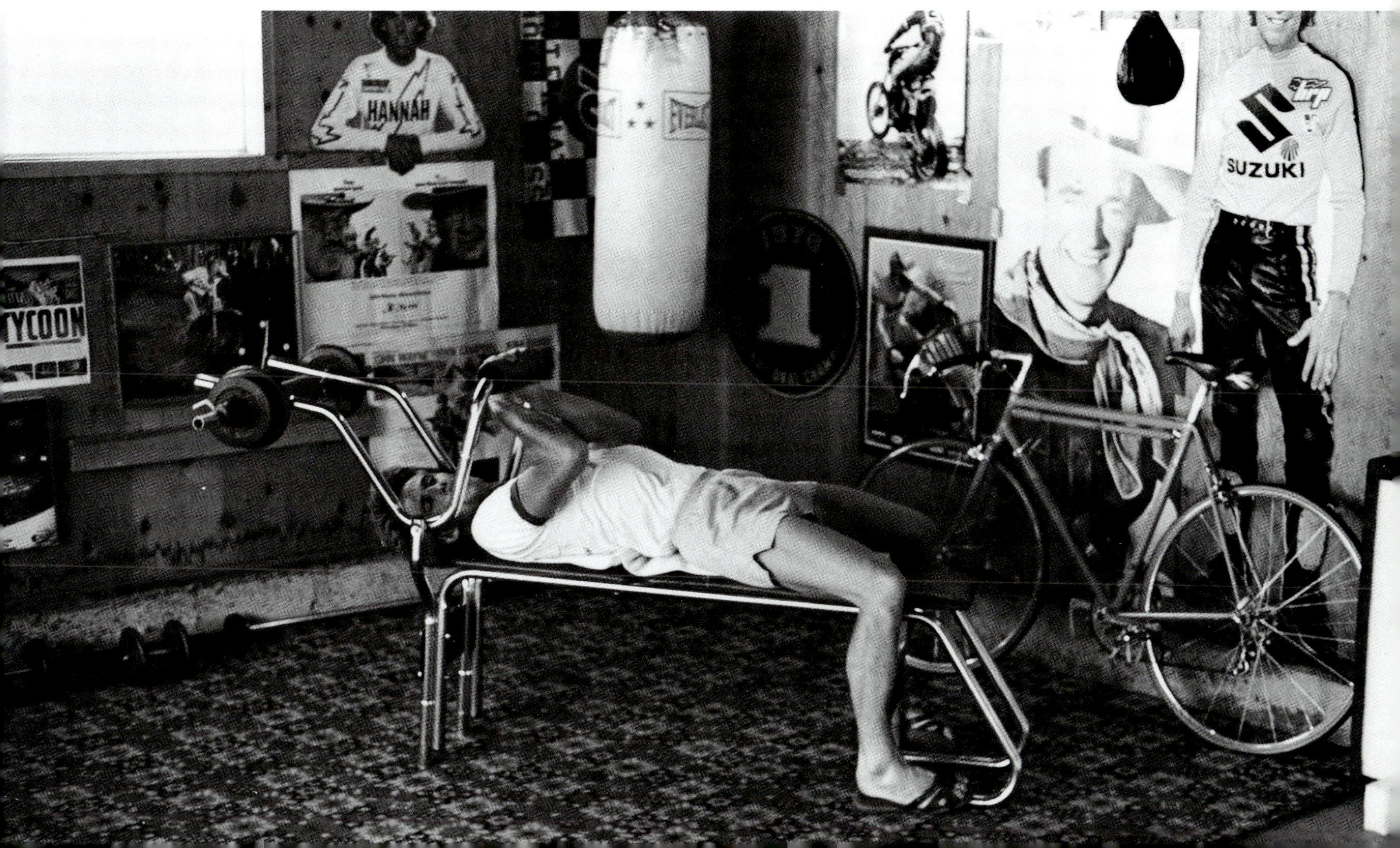

Aside from the 125cc Nationals in 1976, I raced several of the 250cc Nationals, a couple of Supercross races, as well as a few 500cc Nationals and the Trans-AMA series. As a matter of fact, I won the last Trans-AMA 500cc race of the year at Phoenix. The field was filled with Europeans but the track was my style, hard-packed dirt and extremely fast. Roger DeCoster got second. Lucky for me I didn't let the fact that I beat the Europeans go to my head. Those guys were tough and I knew I couldn't beat them on a regular basis; I had gotten a break. My theory was proven at Axton, Virginia.

I got the holeshot and took the lead. Roger had fallen down in the first lap. I led the race until the last lap when Roger, who had come from last place through the field, caught me and passed for the win. When he caught me, I just moved over. I said to myself, "This is ridiculous. I'm not going to fight this guy." He had just come from last to first, so there was no reason to block him. He was faster. I have always believed that if you are not going the same speed as the leader, then get your ass out of the way. All you are is a roadblock, so get the hell out of the road.

Roger DeCoster and Bob Hannah clashed in Europe in the Motocross des Nations and in the United States in the Trans-AMA. DeCoster was a superstar for Team Suzuki and did not take kindly to being beaten by the new kid on the Yamaha. *Steve Reyes*

I didn't know it at the time, but Roger and I, within a year from that first meeting, would become fierce competitors. I would learn a great deal from DeCoster, just by watching him ride. I always considered him to be the best. Beating Roger in that Trans-AMA allowed me to believe that I could run with anyone and, if I trained hard, could win any race I entered.

There are two sides to the 1976 125cc Nationals. Side one was the battle with Marty Smith and my effort to prove I could win. On side two, 1976 was a learning experience with a very steep curve. It was my beginning year. I really didn't know anything about pacing myself or riding with consistency. One week I would ride really good, and the next not as good. Bill Buchka really tried to calm me down and show me my mistakes. But, I was young and impatient. I just wasn't consistent.

Early on in the year, I discovered one of my big weaknesses. I learned that I was the world's worst factory-paid rider in the United States when it came to mud. I was a kid who grew up in the desert and learned to race in the perfect weather of Southern California. I had never experienced mud like they have in the East. Mud racing was my weakness, and I swore that there would be no repeat of New Orleans—I would work on my weakness until it was gone. I stayed in Pennsylvania and started riding in the mud. Every day it rained, I went riding. In those days, when it rained nobody wanted to go out. I saw that as my chance to take advantage. For me, it couldn't rain enough. The harder it came down, the better.

You have to learn to use mud. You have to be able to read the flow of mud, the ruts and puddles. You can't teach anyone how to go fast in mud; it is a feeling you have to learn on your own terms. Some guys never do. The weight difference is incredible. You can gain 20 to 200 pounds depending on the type of mud. By the end of the 1976 season, I was the best mud rider in the country, no joke.

Getting back to my battle with Marty Smith, I can't remember the races and places with any type of

In motocross racing, there is no time out, no stopping play, and no calling the game because of weather. *TMP*

accuracy, after all it's been over thirty years and that amount of detail never mattered to me. The real story can be told by Bill Buchka. Bill and a friend of mine named Terry Good put together the whole story with all the details and I know that I can't match that so I'll say my piece and let them tell the real deal.

One thing I do remember was that the press and I didn't see eye to eye on what was happening. As soon as I started winning, the magazines started with this crap about poor Marty Smith and how much trouble he was having trying to ride the Nationals and the World Championship in the same year. I thought it was all bullshit, and I didn't really like what was being written and I started expressing myself when people would interview me. Finally, this one journalist says to me if I wasn't a little nicer to the press that they would quit writing about me.

I told the guy, "If you quit writing about me you'll be writing about second place on back in the field, so you can do what you want."

Hannah had many different looks throughout his career, but he never changed his way of telling people, including the press, what he thought about things. Shown here is Hannah in 1980 *(above)* when he was with Team Yamaha and in 1987 *(right)* with Team Suzuki. *TMP*

Opposite: Although he was famous for his Supercross title and other major victories riding a Kawasaki, "Jammin' Jimmy" Weinert rode for Team Yamaha early in his career. *Steve Reyes*

Frankly, back then I didn't care for the press all that much. They were enamored of Marty Smith, and they didn't know anything about this kid from Lancaster. They weren't sure I was for real.

That problem with the press, which began in 1976 when they pegged me as cocky and rude, has remained a point of contention throughout the years. I say what I think and what I see. Most people don't like that response when they ask a question. It is worse now in a politically correct world. I have never been politically correct, and I don't like people who are. Just say the truth.

By the halfway point in the 1976 125cc series, I was cooking and I may have gotten just a little cocky. I was learning at every race and getting better every week. All that could have been true in the 125 class but when I ran the 250 class I got a pretty good ass whipping. Both Tony DiStefano and Jimmy Weinert were hot and they didn't care who I was; to them I was just another rider in the way.

It was obvious that if I was going to move up I was going to have to do more training, more practicing, and, above all, show more dedication.

There was plenty of drama throughout the '76 season; believe me, it was not fun and games. I had to work as hard as I had ever worked to stay ahead of Marty. He was a great competitor and a sensational rider. There was no way he wanted me to win that championship. We both had bad days and good breaks and I feel we both rode to our limits, and that makes winning pure and simple.

The one thing that does stick in my head about 1976 was the last race of the year. I had already won the title, but Marty and I were still going hot and heavy. During that last race we were handlebar to handlebar for the lead. I went into a corner with a flat front tire and it washed out and I took both of us down. Marty's bike landed on top of him and I ended up on top of him and his bike. I wanted up quick and as a result I stood on top of Marty and his bike to pull my bike up and get going. Marty was not happy with my act as I rode away leaving him in the dirt.

The pivotal point of the 1976 season was not so much winning the championship as much as it was understanding that all of the hard work, the training, and the riding came together. I knew that I might not win all the races, but I could race with anybody. That was, in my mind, a really big deal. It was big because I never felt that way before.

IT BEGINS: THE 1976 125cc AMA OUTDOOR NATIONALS

As Remembered by Bill Buchka and Terry Good

According to Bill Buchka, Hannah began testing the new Yamaha 125cc bike before the Florida series. Together the two men devised their strategy for the upcoming 1976 Outdoor National series. They discussed each of the competitors and how Bob would ride the individual races. Also given attention were Hannah's strong points and weaknesses, the types of tracks to be raced, and what to expect when he lined up next to a particular rider.

Aside from Marty Smith, the two-time 125cc champion and obvious favorite, there was a strong list of riders capable of beating both Smith and Hannah, including Danny "Magoo" Chandler, Mickey Boone, Tim Hart, Warren Reid, Danny LaPorte, John Savitski, and Broc Glover. Northern California's track at Hangtown is long, rugged, and dry, and is capable of putting a rider on the ground in an instant. Hangtown brings out the best in local competitors (privateers), who all want to knock off the factory hotshots and show the team managers how good they are.

For rookie Bob Hannah, Hangtown would be the first real test. The question was, could a kid from the desert who had developed his own style really compete with the best of the best paid riders in his class?

The gate dropped for moto number one, and things did not look promising. Smith checked out and Hannah checked in at the back of the pack. Was it rookie jitters? Then, as the spectators watched in awe, Hannah began picking off the riders in front of him and, by lap nine, did the impossible—he passed the king of 125cc and put Marty Smith in second place.

The crowd was numb as Hannah took the checkered flag.

In moto two, Marty Smith suffered one of the great fears of a rider: his Honda seized and left him stranded on the back side of the very long Hangtown track. Hannah, the kid nobody knew, came home a winner. The great myth had been unraveled; Marty Smith could be beaten.

From Hangtown, California, the motocross circus moved to Buchanan "Red Bud," Michigan, on May 23. New names appeared on the list of riders who wanted a piece of either Marty Smith or Bob Hannah: John Savitski, Bruce McDougal, Tim Hart, and Mike Kiedrowski headed the list.

The race at Red Bud in 1976 would prove to be another of Hannah's pivitol moments. There must have been shock waves of dread passing through the minds of Team Honda as Red Bud unfolded.

In moto one, Hannah and Smith picked up where their duel in the dirt had left off at Hangtown, but the Honda faltered and Hannah took the first race. In moto two, it was again a handlebar-to-handlebar struggle, and again the Yamaha and Hannah took the victory. Dave Arnold, Marty Smith's mechanic, talked about a clutch problem in moto one, and in the second moto Arnold came to the conclusion that both Marty and Bob rode their hearts out in an effort to prove to each other that they could win. In Arnold's words, "I believe that both Marty and Bob were trying to make a statement."

Opposite: Hannah did not make many close friendships with other riders, but one exception was Danny LaPorte. LaPorte won the 1979 AMA 500cc Outdoor National Championship, rode on the American team that won the Motocross des Nations in 1981, and ran in long-distance races like the Baja 1000 and the Paris-to-Dakar Rally. *TMP*

Hannah's victory at Red Bud may have been a statement, but a privateer named Mickey Boone was about to make an even bigger statement.

According to an AMA regulation, any rider in a race could claim any other rider's bike that was in the same race. To claim Hannah's Yamaha Factory OW27 works bike, Boone simply had to post a $2,500 bond.

To say that panic set in at team Team Yamaha would be an understatement. The idea of the 0W27 falling into the hands of a private rider sent the factory boys into full-on cardiac arrest. Bill Buchka talked about being caught off guard. That was another understatement on the situation. At any rate, there was a thirty-minute time period after the race during which claims could be issued. Two minutes before the deadline, after cashing in traveler's checks and collecting cash from Yamaha engineers and his crew chief Bill Buchka, Hannah filed a claim on his own bike. Drama reached a fever pitch as track officials began to feel the heat from Yamaha and the other factory teams. If it could happen to Yamaha, it could happen to any of the teams. The rules also stated that if there was more than one claim, then the numbers used for drawing starting positions in the motos were to be placed in a hat and the person drawing the highest number got the claim.

Hannah was totally off the chart with anxiety as he voiced his objections for all to hear. The bike was his, set up for him and he didn't want anyone else to have it. His protests fell on deaf ears. So, in typical Hannah fashion, he screamed at Boone, "Draw!"

According to Buchka, Mickey drew a 42 and Bob pulled out a 47. Hannah got his bike, but the idea that a factory bike could be claimed by someone else sent nightmare shivers through the halls at Yamaha, Honda, Suzuki, and the other teams.

By round three at Midland, Michigan, both Honda and Yamaha factories had hit the panic button. Yamaha, fearing that another claim on their super-new water-cooled 0W27/125 would be devastating, decided to pull the bike from competition and instructed Bill Buchka to run the 1976 0W27 chassis with a 1975 works air-cooled motor built by Ed Schiedler. Honda did the same, forcing Smith and Arnold to race a modified production 125cc Elsinore. Suzuki followed, pulling their works bikes too.

At Midland, the Smith vs. Hannah battle picked up with a vengeance. In moto one, the pair went nose to tail, with Smith out front and Hannah dogging him. Eventually, Marty had a partial get-off in one of the corners, allowing Hannah to get past and take the win.

In moto two, the duel was between Bob Hannah and Don Kudaiski. Both were excellent sand riders, and Midland was a track that featured a considerable amount of sand. Halfway through moto two, Hannah's works monoshock began to fade and, after a couple of near crashes and a not-yet-invented feet-in-the-air "Superman" flyaway, Bob decided to roll back on the throttle and settle for second, gathering enough points for the overall win.

Bill Buchka and Hannah were still feeling stress from the possibility of losing the water-cooled OW27 model. So, in reaction to the episode at Red Bud, Yamaha supplied the team with a disclaimer letter stating in part that they would not be able to supply parts or support to anyone who might claim one of their bikes. The factory also supplied the team with money to use against anyone else's claim on one of their bikes.

Yamaha, Suzuki, Honda, and Kawasaki were all fighting hard to gain a foothold in the American motorcycle marketplace, and winning motocross races sold product. Suzuki had several superstars including Roger DeCoster and Billy Grossi (shown here) to do battle with Yamaha's Hurricane. *Steve Reyes*

On July 4, 1976 (America's 200th birthday), the series moved to Keyser's Ridge, Maryland. The pits were buzzing about this kid from California who was kicking Honda's ass. An unknown leading the championship was the ultimate insult to the veteran factory riders. The talk was that Hannah was a three-race wonder and would soon be out of the picture.

Keyser's Ridge is a beautiful place nestled in the Allegheny Mountains. But the track's natural beauty was overlooked since the claiming threat was still a worry to the works teams. This situation overshadowed the whole series. The factories were caught between a rock and a hard place. If they ran a factory works bike and it was claimed, their secrets would be exposed. If they didn't run a works bike, the other teams could beat them for the championship. Honda decided to run the works bike for Marty Smith. Hannah ran his modified "Buchka Pounder."

Hannah's luck ran out in moto one. He fell at the start of the race, but said later, "I wasn't too worried because I knew I could work my way back to the front." But, then he threw a chain and had to stop and do an on-track fix. Finally, the crankshaft broke, leaving Hannah a spectator to Smith's victory. More worrisome was the loss of twenty-five points.

Moto two saw Steve Wise take the win, with Marty second and Hannah third. The overall win went to Smith, and Hannah got twentieth overall. The whispers started: "Hannah is human after all."

The factory teams found a way to counterattack the claiming rule. When someone posted a claim on a factory bike, the teams and the support riders, crew members, and engineers—in short, anyone connected to the team—would post claims too, giving the factory better odds of winning the bike back. According to Hannah, the whole idea of claiming a factory bike sucked.

The second week of July found the series in Lexington, Ohio, for the 125cc USGP round of the World Championship. Because the race was sanctioned by the Federation Internationale de Motocyclisme (FIM) and part of the world title chase, there would be no claiming rule. Team Yamaha had Hannah back on the water-cooled 0W27. Dave Arnold and Marty Smith put together a brand new factory works bike for the USGP, hoping to give Hannah a riding lesson.

Hannah took time away from his run for the Supercross title in 1979 to run a 125cc Yamaha at the Mid-Ohio USGP. *Werner Straub; Terry Good*

Marty had been running in both Europe and the United States, trying to win the National title as well as the World Championship. Lexington was a track suited to Smith, and there were several new players that could become roadblocks to Hannah's wide-open, hard-charging style. Leading the pack of contenders was 125cc World Champion Gaston Rahier, who was going for a second title, and Yoshifumo Sugia, the Japanese champion who was riding a duplicate works bike to that of Hannah.

In moto one, Smith took the holeshot. Hannah followed, and the pair picked up where they had left off, handlebar to handlebar. Marty was on his game, and after the two swapped the lead several times, Smith took it for good. Hannah had a problem and, after the moto, told his mechanic, "The brake cable had looped over the forks and put the front brake on. I couldn't ride like that. It happened in fourth gear and I started tank-slapping and had to back off and let Marty past." Hannah managed to finish second.

In moto two things got ugly. Marty got the holeshot and Hannah started third, but quickly moved to second. Hannah forced his way past Smith on lap two. Then Billy Grossi joined the fight and, according to Bill Buchka, the three riders put on a show that had the fans whipped into a frenzy. Then Smith decided he was going to take command. He forced his way under Hannah and, when Bob missed a shift, Marty said, "See ya!" Marty won, with Bob second.

Hannah later admitted that Marty had ridden a great race and had beaten him fair and square. For Smith, it was his first GP victory of the year and it would help his charge toward the U.S. Outdoor National title.

After the USGP, Bill Buchka confided that Hannah told him, "I have to have the OW27 if you want me to maintain my lead in the championship." Buchka agreed and relayed the message to Yamaha. The decision was made: Yamaha would run the works bike at round five in Delta, Ohio, claiming rule or not.

In 1978, Keith McCarty assembled a Yamaha 125cc bike from spare parts and the team went to the USGP at Mid-Ohio. *Werner Straub; Terry Good*

At Delta, both Honda and Yamaha rolled out full-on works bikes, with Honda unpacking their new Type-2 125. Dave Arnold remarked that Marty liked the new bike and felt ready to take the war to the Yamaha camp.

Hannah on the other hand didn't say much to anyone, especially the press. He was totally committed to the job to be done and, when he got like that, his mood became sullen and quiet.

When the starting gate dropped for the first moto, Warren Reid, on a Honda, made a holeshot blast for the lead, with Husky rider Ario Englund in second, then Glover and Smith. Hannah got tangled up with several backmarkers and was relegated to the rear of the pack. Marty Smith unloaded the full potential of his new Honda and took over the lead. He proceeded to open a fourteen-second margin between him and

Hannah, who had blown by the backmarkers and into second place. As Smith came up to lap a pair of slower riders, one of the two decided to race Smith and, when he did, a case of brain fade set in. The backmarker collected Marty and the pair hit the dirt. Hannah smoked past the helpless Smith and took the win. Broc Glover finished second.

There was a feeling of bitterness and outrage in the Honda pits. Smith was overheard saying that the incident may have cost him the championship. Getting taken down by a backmarker for no reason is something that neither Smith nor Hannah wanted to happen. In the second moto, Marty vented his frustrations by running over the competition and won going away. But, like a bad dream—a nightmare that you can't wake up from—Hannah finished second and took the overall win with a 1-2 score. Smith finished fourth with a 10-1.

August 15th in San Antonio, Texas, marked another one of those pivotal points in Bob Hannah's career. Sporting long, shaggy hair, a confident smirk, and a genuine dislike for the rest of the field, Hannah reached a new plateau as a professional motocross rider.

The enthusiast magazine *Motocross Action* may have put everything into the proper perspective when a headline read "The Day the Hurricane Blew Old Dixie Down." Hannah would prove his ability and toughness once and for all.

The claiming rule again plagued the field at San Antonio when a young racer's father stated he would claim Hannah's bike, the water-cooled OW27. Although it only turned out to be a threat, it was a move that, plain and simple, pissed off Yamaha and Hannah. "Let him claim it," said the Hurricane. "Then let him try and get it." But, it was still a risk and, in the eyes of the teams, it was just dumb. Honda blinked and pulled their new Type 2 bike from Marty's hands and gave him and Dave Arnold a Type 1. Hannah, known throughout the pits for having a very caustic mouth, commented that anyone claiming his bike would have to find it. "Screw that guy if he thinks he's getting my bike," barked Hannah, loud enough for all to hear.

Heat, from the blistering Texas sun, was the biggest concern for the field. The air temperature, according to Bill Buchka, was about 108 degrees Fahrenheit on the track surface.

Anyone who really knows Bob Hannah will tell you that when it comes to beating the competition, he is without mercy, pity, or compassion. If you happen to be a weak sucker and show any signs of backing down, Hannah will delight in destroying you. If you puke from the heat, Bob will laugh. Hands full of blisters? Too bad! When your lungs scream for air, his comment would be, "Should have trained harder."

Every time things got so bad he would feel like quitting, Hannah simply remembered his episode of heat exhaustion in New Orleans in 1975 and the whipping he took, and it made him grab a gear and put the throttle on "kill." In fact, at this point, he was working himself into perfect condition. No white sugar, no junk food, no booze. He trained until his muscles cried in pain. Then he went harder. Hannah once remarked that you had to love a track, all its ruts and holes, off-camber turns, hills, and mud. Embrace the pain; push the rider ahead of you; no mercy, and no love. Bob would remember his dad and the warning, "If you fall off, you can't ride anymore."

Bob Hannah had developed a mean streak; he was a junkyard dog on the track, biting anyone who came near. The heat, dust, and rugged track of San Antonio allowed Hannah to put his ugly side on display. According to Buchka, Hannah simply rode a steady pace and the rest of the field just couldn't keep up.

He was now the "Hurricane" in truth and in deed and, at San Antonio, Hannah had proven his point. He won both motos and, for all practical purposes, had a death grip on the 125cc Outdoor National title.

When the Nationals rolled into Houston, Texas, Yamaha had a substantial points lead and it looked like a rookie kid from California would be champion. Honda showed up with their Type 2 version of the 125, ignoring the chance of a claim. Honda figured that if they didn't show big they would lose face. Broc Glover was the hero of moto one. Bob and his mechanic decided not to take any chances, so Hannah was satisfied with second. During moto two, the same mind set was displayed by Buchka and Hannah. In fact, at one point during moto two, Bob actually waved Marty Smith past, something that didn't set well with the Honda rider. Hannah ended the moto in fourth with Smith in fifth. Hurricane Bob Hannah was the 1976 125cc National Champion. It was his first championship and triggered his first bonus from Yamaha.

Bill Buchka offered his personal comments about winning the title. He said, "We celebrated with pizza and beer. It was the first time anyone on the team had seen Bob drink anything but water, iced tea, fruit juice, or Gatorade. Two beers and he fell on his ass. The guys ribbed him pretty hard; it was meant to keep his feet on the ground at this early stage in his career. He was still just a kid."

Two things were of great importance concerning the last race of the 1976 National season in New Orleans. Hannah would not repeat his 1975 debacle, and he would not take the race lightly. As if to prove his point about his conditioning, Hannah smoked the field in moto one, running away from his buddy Danny LaPorte, Glover, Smith, Wise, and Turner. Moto two turned from a runaway for Hannah into a barn-burner. At the start, Hannah and LaPorte went at each other like two scalded cats. LaPorte rode his Suzuki like he stole it, and Hannah didn't like being challenged. The two banged bars and exchanged a few looks. After Hannah dispatched LaPorte, Smith took his turn.

Smith had something to prove. The fans could sense that the whole frustrating year was coming to a close and the two-time champion, the boy wonder of motocross, the one who some believed could not be beaten, was about to lose his golden image. He wanted to show the world that he could still be the best. He didn't want the cocky kid from the desert to take his championship without one last knockout fight. With only a few laps to go, Smith had come from a long way back to catch Hannah and the two went side by side.

Then it happened the way anyone who loves a great story will tell you it had to happen—the two warriors collided. Smith went down first, with Hannah on top. For several seconds the two combatants lay in a heap. Hannah, as if to show the other riders that he was not to be messed with, grabbed his bike while standing on top of Smith, yanked it upright and took off. Marty was furious about being stepped on and let his feelings be heard after the race. Danny LaPorte won the moto, but Hannah finished second overall.

With the conclusion of the 1976 125cc National Championship in his hands, Bob Hannah had completed a phenomenal year. Not only did he win the 125cc National Championship series, but also the 500cc Open Florida Winter Series, one 250cc National, and one Trans-AMA race. Bob Hannah was a force to be reckoned with.

In 1978, Bob Hannah was the first American rider to win the Trans-AMA Championship. He is shown here at the Mid-Ohio Trans-AMA event on the OW-39 Yamaha. *Werner Straub; Terry Good*

As a footnote to the 1976 season, Bill Buchka would leave his position as Hannah's mechanic and go to Europe. Marty Smith would go on to be a superstar in Supercross, the 250cc Outdoor National series, and the 500cc Outdoor National series. Danny LaPorte, Broc Glover, Steve Wise, Warren Reid, John Savitski, Billy Grossi, and Ron Turner would all go on to become stars in Supercross and continue to be competitors determined to control the Hurricane.

Known as an aggressive rider throughout his career, Hannah claimed that he would never start problems, only finish them. He said, "If a rider comes up behind me and is faster, I feel that I should get out of the way. When I come up on slower riders, I expect the same response. If I don't get respect, I'll move them out of the way." *TMP*

Bob Hannah riding for Team Suzuki in 1987. *TMP*

4

IN THE EYE OF THE STORM: FRIENDS AND MEMORIES

KING OF THE STICKERS

Ken Boyko, a longtime friend of Bob Hannah, was involved in many interesting moments during the early years of Bob's career. He was anxious to offer some of his recollections of watching a wild kid raised in the desert rise to become a national hero.

KEN BOYKO

My career in motorcycle racing actually began with minibikes. I had been working for an aftermarket company, specializing in racing parts for minibikes, called Myerscough Machine Company. My tenure there was short-lived, however. When the owner's son, Brian, signed a professional riding contract with Suzuki, the elder Myerscough sold the business and I was out of a job. Not wanting to remain unemployed, I approached the owner of another aftermarket company called DG Performance. Gary Harlow, the founder of DG Performance, was very open-minded and took an aggressive posture toward new ideas. My proposal was to start a minibike racing team carrying the DG logo. Harlow bought the idea, and within six months I was promoted to handle sales and promotion for the entire line of DG products.

In the course of my duties at DG I became familiar with a young rider named Bob Hannah who was in and out of the shop on a regular basis. I learned that Hannah had ridden for Gary before he signed the factory deal with Yamaha. There was gossip that Harlow had played a very prominent part in Hannah getting a contract with Yamaha.

Having a colorful helmet emblazoned with his famed lightning bolts began back in the 1970s. Hannah was one of the first riders to get paid for putting sponsor endorsements on his helmet. *mxworksbike.com*

The one thing I noticed from my very early dealings with Hannah was the fact that he would ride with a DG emblem on his jersey. Back in the mid-1970s, factory riders didn't have sponsors. They rode for the factory, and the idea of personal sponsorship endorsements was discouraged. The practice was rare, but Bob made himself an exception. By 1978, Hannah was a hero at Yamaha and he did, pretty much, whatever he wanted to do.

Manufacturers wanted to be involved with the Hurricane, and Hannah welcomed the opportunity to promote sponsors he liked. At one point, I became "king of the stickers." It was my job to make sure that when Bob Hannah came to the starting line, his sponsor logos could be seen clearly. I remember that Bob had DG, Goodyear Tires, Scott Goggles, Bell Helmets, and several others. Cleaning mud and replacing stickers was my appointment between motos. To my knowledge, Bob Hannah was the first rider to show up with his helmet decked out in decals, plus he added his signature lightning bolts as part of his image. He started the custom helmet graphics trend.

It is impossible to be around Bob Hannah without gathering a lifetime of stories centered on his racing career. It would fill volumes to tell his entire memoir. He was just as colorful off the track as he was on, and those are the depictions few people really know. I have three favorite stories and I think they offer an accurate view of Hannah's character.

First is a portrait of how much influence Hannah had on the sport. He actually changed the style of riding gear long before it was cool to be stylin'. In the late '70s, riders all used a nylon perforated jersey that would rub on the riders' skin so hard that they would have to wear Band-Aids over their nipples. Anyway, Hannah came into Gary Harlow's office at DG in 1978 with a stack of nylon jerseys for us so we could sew DG patches on them. His sister, Tammy, was the official patch installer but for some reason she couldn't do this batch. Hannah was bitchin' and moanin' about how these jerseys tore up his chest and how he had to wear Band-Aids on his tits.

Now, at the time, DG made a long-sleeve, 100 percent cotton jersey for off-track use that Bob wore all the time. When he started complaining about the nylon riding shirts, Gary said, "What would you like?" Bob said, "This," and he pointed to his long-sleeve T-shirt. He then told us that he had been riding practice with the shirts and he loved them. So, I went down to a local JCPenney store and bought six yellow long-sleeve T-shirts. We then took the shirts down to our screen printer and had him screen "Yamaha" on the front, "Hannah" and his number on the back, and add DG, Goodyear, Scott, Bell, and who ever else he had at the time. It was four days before the Hangtown National. On the morning of tech inspection, I showed up with the shirts and Hannah was freaking out—he loved them. The color was not the official Yamaha yellow, so when Bob flashed his new shirt to the team manager, the guy just shook his head and walked off. At that point in his career, Hannah was winning everything in sight and Yamaha would let him get away with whatever he wanted to do.

Bob wore the jersey in the race. The Monday morning after the race the phone was ringing off the hook with orders for Hannah riding shirts. DG was a hard parts supplier and not an apparel manufacturer, so for the next six months we ordered twelve boxes of yellow long-sleeve T-shirts from JCPenney per week. As fast as we could print them, they were out the door. Finally, Gary made a deal with an apparel maker to supply DG with Hannah shirts.

My second-favorite story happened in 1978 one night after the race at Red Bud in Michigan. A bunch of us went to dinner at some steak house and Bob's buddy Bevo was at the table. It is safe to say that back then Bob and Bevo were capable of doing the most outlandish stunts imaginable. Bevo had ordered a huge prime rib and after he finished there was a huge slab of fat left over. Bob pulls out a hundred dollar bill and bets Bevo that if he can swallow the fat in one gulp he'll give him the hundred bucks. Bevo grabs the fat and tries but it doesn't go and he coughs up and the chunk goes flying and lands at the table next to us. Hannah yells, "Check!"

Finally, everyone thinks of Bob as a hard-nosed tough guy who is not always politically correct, and the press sometimes gives him a bad rap. Bob is just not the kind of person who will tell anyone about all the good stuff he does.

Roger DeCoster was to Suzuki what the Hurricane was to Yamaha, a hard-charging winner with a colorful personality. *Steve Reyes*

There is one incident that I will never forget. It was after Bob won the Supercross in Dallas in '78. It was a mud-fest and raining so hard you couldn't see five feet. Bob was really beat up after the race, so he said to me, "Here are the keys to my rental car. Back it down the tunnel and I'll jump in and we can take off."

It was about an hour after the race and Bob decided it was time to leave. I had the car backed into the tunnel and he jumped in with his jacket pulled up so nobody could recognize him and we headed out. Just as we exited the tunnel, there were a couple hundred fans standing in the rain waiting for Hannah to show up. He said, "Pull over!" Bob got out of the car and sat with the fans in the pouring rain signing autographs. He was so loyal to his fans, and that's what made him so popular. Hannah and Roger DeCoster were two guys who would never say no to a kid who wanted an autograph after a race.

Although he never made it an issue to the press, Hannah loved those kids. When it came to a friend or a young fan, the Hurricane would always be there. There is no compromise with Bob Hannah. He loves his friends and he hates his enemies. No gray area.

Two old friends and racing competitors are shown talking about the old days. Throughout Hannah's career, Eddie Cole (left) has been a huge supporter and friend. Cole and Hannah raced each other in the early years, they roomed together when neither had any money, and later Eddie created Answer Products and became one of Bob's major sponsors. *TMP*

HOW ABOUT A NEW FERRARI?

Today, Eddie Cole is a very successful businessman who owns a company called Valencia Sport Group, but in the early 1970s he was a struggling motocross racer; young and wild and racing for the fun of it. Cole began racing against Bob Hannah long before either one ever even thought it possible to get a factory ride. In the end, Hannah got the brass ring and Cole turned to manufacturing racing products. His company at that time, Answer Products, became a giant in the American motocross scene and was a major sponsor throughout Bob Hannah's career.

In 2007, Eddie Cole sat down and talked about those early days and his friendship with the Hurricane over the years.

EDDIE COLE

The first time I really met and talked to Bob was at the old Indian Dunes Motorcycle Park in Valencia, California. He had some type of a development program with Suzuki and was riding test bikes at local events. This was before he signed with Yamaha in late 1975. I was riding for Bultaco as a factory-paid rider. I was scheduled to ride the Nationals, the Trans-AMA series, and several local events. Actually, I had been a factory rider from 1974, when I rode the Nationals for Kawasaki. At that time, Bob was still out in the desert racing pucker bushes. At any rate, over a period of time we became friends as well as competitors.

After Bob signed with Yamaha in late 1975, he was getting ready to run the Florida Winter Series. I remember I had a bad knee and was on crutches—not looking good for the upcoming season. Hannah said, "Come on, Eddie, we're going to Yamaha."

He marched into the president's office and said, "We need to get Eddie some bikes for next season." The next thing I know, I'm in Florida riding a Yamaha on a privateer deal. Bob and I were roommates throughout the series and, at the end of six or eight weeks, became good friends. Hannah won the series; it was a sign of things to come.

During that 1976 season I ran the 125cc class in the Nationals. I hurt my knee again and my career was looking on the downhill side. It was just the opposite for Bob, as he won the 125cc Championship as a rookie and his career was off and running.

During this same time period, a friend of mine and I started a company called Answer Products. We each put in a hundred bucks and worked out of my partner's garage. Our first products were a Bultaco swingarm and a Bob Hannah-signature practice starting gate. Soon after beginning, we introduced a line of signature handlebars by riders including Rick Burgett, Brad Lackey, and Bob Hannah. The bars were very unique—they were copies of the actual bends each rider used on his factory works bike. It was the first time amateur riders could ride with pro bars. As business grew, we would continually add name riders to the list. Within months the business took off and we could hardly keep bars in stock. Our deal with the riders was that we paid them 50 cents a bar.

One American rider who put the United States in the world motocross spotlight was Brad Lackey. Lackey was 1972 AMA 500cc Outdoor National Champion and World 500cc Champion in 1982. *Steve Reyes*

Hannah bars started flying off the shelves, and the more he won, the more bars we sold.

Bob, who kept very close tabs on every penny he had coming, would stop by after every series and say, "Eddie, how many bars did we sell?" I didn't have a clue. Our bookkeeping system consisted of one box for money in and one box for bills to be paid. I would tell Bob, "I owe you, but I don't have any money." He would just laugh and take us to dinner.

This went on for a while and finally we started making money and I decided to settle up with Bob. I waited and when Bob showed up I told him, "Hey, we're making some money and I know you just moved into a house in Sun Valley so I would like to buy you something nice."

I was thinking microwave, big screen TV, or dishwasher. Hannah said, "Cool, my contract with John Gregory at JT is up and he took back the Ferrari he had been loaning me, so how about a new Ferrari?"

Under my breath I said, "Oh crap, now what?"

At the time I had a division of my company called Answer Euro located in Italy managed by an ex-motocross champion named Dario Nanni who knew people at Ferrari. Dario got me a deal on a 308. It was shipped to Phoenix, to a local dealership owned by a wild man named Harley Cluxton. I sent Bob to Phoenix with a cover story that I wanted to pick up some parts. Harley picked Bob up in a Bell Ranger helicopter and flew him to the dealership to get his Ferrari.

By 1978, Answer Products expanded into a line of race wear, expansion chambers, and all types of racing products. Hannah was a major supporter, and he wore and used our products until the end of his career at Suzuki. We even supplied products for his personal line, Hannah Racing Products, until it dissolved.

There are two very distinctive sides to Hannah's personality. He has thousands of fans and acquaintances but very few close friends. He tells people what he thinks, and he never backs down. Most people don't realize that Hannah came from nothing, and everything he got, he earned. He made a living racing motorcycles, and the demands to win made him tough and fearsome to his competitors. Nobody was more serious than Bob Hannah at the starting gate.

The flip side of his character is his ability to have fun. Off the track, anything could happen and this book needs some fun so, as a friend, I can share several memories that still crack me up to this day.

The famed lightning bolts began back in the 1970s and carried over from Yamaha to Honda. Hannah was also one of the first riders to get paid for wearing sponsor endorsements on his helmet. *TMP*

During that first winter series in Florida in 1976, we had time on our hands looking for something to do. There was a large parking lot for a local mall about a block from our hotel. One day, at dusk, when the parking lot was empty, Bob decided that he was going to hang on to the side of a rental car while riding a bicycle and try to catch one of the many sea gulls that squatted in the lot after the place emptied out. We made about ten passes at about fifty miles per hour with Hannah hanging on to the car, trying to catch a sea gull. It was a wonder that his career didn't end in that parking lot.

Another time, several of the teams went to a local go-kart track for some off-night fun. It didn't take long before things got out of hand. Hannah was racing someone from Suzuki, and he accidentally hit one of the innocent customers, a young girl, and sent her kart flying off the track. The manager came roaring down and said, "That's it, you jokers are out of here." Hannah told the manager that he would like to buy the track, right on the spot, so we could all keep racing.

Action from the 1987 AMA 250cc National at Hangtown as Hannah shows his classic style on the Suzuki. *Hannah*

Action photographer and contributor to this book, Steve Reyes, took time off from his usual beat shooting NHRA drag races and captured a mud-covered Hannah during a 1977 AMA 250cc Outdoor National event. *Steve Reyes*

My final story happened in Sun Valley, Idaho. Bob's buddy Bevo and I were there and Hannah decided we were going fishing at some secret spot that only he knew about. We all piled into Bob's Toyota pickup truck and got ready to take off. Now, just in case you are uninformed, Bevo is a very big guy and things were tight as we crammed into the truck. Bob always wanted to bet on something, anything, it didn't matter. So, Bob said, "Hey, I'll bet you guys five bucks I can get all the way to the fishing hole without lifting off the throttle. I'll drive WFO and never lift."

Like idiots, we took the bet.

Suddenly, we were flying up this fire road sliding sideways with rocks hitting the fenders. Sure enough, in typical Hannah fashion, we stayed flat out for about five miles, Bevo cussing and Bob laughing all the way. It was the wildest ride of my life.

I think that Bob uses his wild side as a way to release stress and challenge his friends.

We have remained friends throughout the years and, to this day, if I ask Bob for a favor or to make an appearance to help promote my business, he will do it. I know taking time from his private life and his own business is something he hates doing, but he is loyal to his friends and that is more important to him than any inconvenience.

DON'T WASH IT, DON'T TOUCH IT, IT'S READY TO RACE

The person who played the most consequential role in Bob Hannah's motocross racing career was his mechanic from 1977 to 1982, Keith McCarty. He had the same drive and determination as Hannah and was just as obsessed with winning. It was during his tenure as mechanic that Bob Hannah enjoyed his greatest moments. McCarty took over for Hannah's first Yamaha mechanic, Bill Buchka, after the 1976 season and Hannah's first championship. McCarty remains at Yamaha as race director and is still close friends with Hannah. Keith agreed to offer some of his memories in an interview conducted in 2007.

KEITH MCCARTY

The very first time I met Bob Hannah was in 1975 at Suzuki. I was the mechanic for Tony DiStefano, and Bob was on the Suzuki support program riding local races. Then, sometime in 1976, I was approached by the supervisor of Yamaha racing about joining the Yamaha team. I had won two championships with Tony D and had a good reputation for getting the job done so Yamaha was interested in what I had to offer.

Opposite: The hard-charging "Tony D," Tony DiStefano, won the AMA 250cc Outdoor National Championship three years in a row (1975–1977) on a Suzuki before Hannah and McCarty took the title in 1978 and 1979 on a Yamaha. *Steve Reyes*

TONY
BELL
HELMETS
FULL HOUSE
SUZUKI
76

Often at odds with Hannah, five-time world champion Roger DeCoster won the U.S. Trans-Am title four years straight before losing to the Hurricane in 1978. *Steve Reyes*

Because Bill Buchka, Bob's mechanic, was leaving for Yamaha in Europe, Bob had given Yamaha three names as replacements. I was one of them.

However, the real turning point to me making a decision materialized at the conclusion of the Trans-Am series. DiStefano wanted to make some changes that I didn't agree with concerning using aftermarket fenders on our race bikes. He had a deal with Preston Petty Fenders and I didn't want to use them. It was a small issue, but it was part of some other things going on and, in the end, I left Suzuki.

I started at Yamaha on January 3, 1977. Shortly after I joined Yamaha, Bob and I left for the Florida winter series. We ran a Yamaha YZ250D production bike, the only problem being that I had not even seen the bike. Bob had been in Japan testing the new bikes and did not return until a few days before the series was to start. I had to spend several days and nights learning the bike from scratch. Lucky for both of us, we were compatible when it came to preparation, and Bob told me exactly what he needed. The results were twelve straight victories and the series championship.

It was obvious to me that Hannah had something special in talent, but no one could have predicted how his career would explode into legend.

As we became more acclimated with working together, I would classify Bob as an angry individual. He was very hurt by Suzuki's rejection when he had asked to ride the Nationals and they declined. Then, when Yamaha offered him a contract and he asked Suzuki to match it, they laughed, and that touched something inside that really set him off.

He was angry at the competition because he wanted to win so bad that he couldn't accept losing. He wanted to beat every rider, and beat them by the widest margin possible. He would even mock some of the riders about how little effort they put out. He wondered how they could take home a paycheck.

Bob had a very small circle of friends and tried to play his life low-key. His dislike for other riders created problems in the press, and he was misquoted on a regular basis. He never attempted to change anyone's opinion of him, ignoring what was said about him.

In 1977 we raced all three classes: 125cc, 250cc, and open 500cc. The challenges were many because, at the time, Yamaha didn't have a big organization and every person was on their own. I had to learn about all three bikes instantly. Aside from learning the three classes, there was the difference in politics between Suzuki and Yamaha.

These two old friends have a twenty-nine year history of working together. Keith McCarty and Bob Hannah began as a team in 1977, won many races together, brought Yamaha seven titles, and brought motocross racing front and center in the United States. Great friends for many years, the warriors met up again in 2007 at the AMA Superbike race at Laguna Seca (bottom). *Hannah*

We had issues, but still gave a good account of our efforts. I believe that Bob could have won all three classes had we not developed some bike problems. Then, Bob won in Atlanta; Daytona Beach; Dallas, Texas; two nights at the Pontiac Silverdome; and Anaheim, California, to capture the Supercross Championship.

Bob took second in the Trans-Am series, behind Roger DeCoster. In the 125cc class, we had some problems, including team orders to allow Broc Glover to pass so he could win the title. It should be noted that Bob won more races than Broc, three out of six, and finished third in the final standings. Tony DiStefano won the 250cc Nationals. Hannah finished second to Marty Smith in the 500cc class.

The Hurricane blew at full strength in 1978. The AMA class structure changed in '78, and we became more specialized, staying with the 250cc for most of the season. We won the Florida series, the Supercross series, and the 250cc National title. Bob won the Trans-Am series on a 500cc open bike. I think we won about 70 to 80 percent of all the races we ran. At one point, Hannah posted a twenty-two-straight moto win streak. At the Pontiac Silverdome double header, Bob won both nights and a fan brought out hurricane warning flags and put them up in the stadium. Hannah became the fans' favorite, and he put Yamaha on the motocross map.

As a sidebar to this story, Bob and I went to Germany in 1978 for the Motocross des Nations. It was an opportunity for Bob to show the Europeans what he could do. Unfortunately we had to overcome the fact that Yamaha had sent us a YZ250 works bike in a crate with very few extra parts, and we had almost no time for practice. Bob felt that if we would have had more practice time, he could have done better. He got a fifth in the first moto, with DeCoster finishing sixth. In the second moto, Bob finished second behind Heikki Mikkola. The U.S. Team finished fourth in the final standings.

Overall, Bob didn't like Europe; the food, the weather, he couldn't do the things he liked. However, he did take one valuable lesson home and that was a newfound respect for riders like Roger DeCoster and Mikkola. In fact, upon our return to America, Bob hung a full-size photo of Mikkola in his gym and used it as an inspiration to induce him to work harder.

By 1979, Bob and I had developed a routine for each race. We knew each other well enough to give the other person what he needed. Bob trained to reach physical perfection, and we tested constantly to a point where I could build a bike to his exact needs. A good example of our pattern would be the first Supercross race of the year at Anaheim.

We never took the chance of doing any preparation at the track. Too many things could go wrong. It was extremely important that when the bike rolled onto a track the first time, everything was ready. So, for Anaheim we got the bike ready then took it into some local hills on the morning of the race and did the final testing. Set in the brakes; the clutch and shock settings; riding position; everything would be perfect. We loaded up and went directly to the track. Maybe the bike was a little dirty, but we never touched a thing. Bob would say, "Don't wash it, don't touch it, it's ready to race."

I would catch flack from our boss about the bike not being perfectly clean. It didn't matter to us. We wanted function.

Obviously Bob rewarded my efforts with wins. Winning was everything to both of us. We were giving up a good part of our lives, and winning was the purpose of our sacrifice. I can promise you that the spoils of victory go to the rider and not the mechanic. So it wasn't the money or fame for me, it was to prove that my hard work could win. I was half of a winning team.

Being on the road was very difficult for me and my family. There were times when Bob and I would be gone for three months at a time. We also didn't have much face time with the Yamaha factory headquarters. This factor developed into a pain-in-the-ass issue. For me, Monday and Tuesday of a race week were normal, but by Thursday things were ramping up and by Friday I got really tense. Then race time would happen and our boss would show up and want to talk about problems.

Opposite: Hannah won his first championship for Yamaha in 1976, taking the 125cc National Title. Bill Buchka was Hannah's mechanic in 1976, then Keith McCarty took over. Hannah and McCarty created another winning combination. *Dennis Kanegae*

YAMAHA
When you know how they're built.

Bob Hannah is the heavy favorite to capture his third consecutive Toyota Supercross series championship

1979

In 1979, Bob Hannah was at the top of his game, riding his best and carrying the Number One plate as 1978 250cc National Champion. Here, the Hurricane unleashes his fury during the 1979 Outdoor National at Saddleback Park. *Terry Good*

I would go bonkers and Bob would get really surly. We hated being distracted and our attitude would get back to headquarters causing concern, but it didn't change our reactions. Talking business or discussing problems on race day just didn't work.

On the road, Hannah kept by himself most of the time and was very serious about training and practice. He got along with his teammate Rick Burgett and with Broc Glover's mechanic Jim Felts, but never warmed up to Glover. As for being a team player, with the exception of allowing Glover to pass him to win the 1977 Championship, Bob didn't like team strategy.

Bob won his first title in 1976 with Bill Buchka. But, from that point on—1977, 1978, 1979—Bob won all of his other championships with me as mechanic. That included the 250cc Nationals in '78 and '79; the Supercross Championship in '77, '78, and '79; and the Trans-Am USA series title in '78. At the end of the 1979 season, Hannah had become the winningest rider in American motocross history. He was kicking ass and taking names. He was one of two golden boys at Yamaha, Kenny Roberts being the other.

At the end of the '79 season, I figured the Hurricane would continue to blow the competition into the weeds and the fun would never end. Then it happened! Bob crashed on water-skis and things got very serious. His leg was shattered and there was talk of amputation. He could very well have lost his leg.

Above: Throughout his career Hannah claimed that his style lacked the smooth lines of some of the other top riders. Those who watched Hannah race would argue he was awesome *because* he rode flat out all the time. *Dennis Kanegae*

Left: In 1978 Bob Hannah was a member of the United States Motocross des Nations team that competed in Gaildorf, Germany. From the left, Hannah is shown here with team members Tommy Croft, Chuck Sun, and Rick Burgett. *Moto Verte; Terry Good*

Bob was off the entire 1980 season, but made his comeback in 1981. In that twelve-month period, things changed. Mike Bell had won the Supercross title in 1980 and he and Broc Glover had developed a race bike that was quite different than the one Bob had left in '79. Both Glover and Bell are larger riders than Bob, and the engineers had designed a bike for them.

I don't know who had the ideas, but they made the bike taller, pushed the front end out longer, and changed the steering, all to accommodate a taller rider. The problem was, when they finished, they had created a bike that even the tall riders couldn't ride. They had sacrificed steering and turning for straightaway performance. They ended up with a bike that went good down a straight, but didn't work in the corners. Bob and I had always built our bikes to turn well, because our philosophy was that you win a race in the corners. Straight line speed didn't matter unless you were fast getting into and out of corners. The bike didn't suit Bob's riding style and he had trouble. As the season began, Bob had to overcome his injuries, both physical and mental. The bike was too heavy, it didn't handle, and we were struggling to turn things around from day one.

The one bright spot of the season happened at Saddleback Park. Kent Howerton had won the 250cc National title in 1980 for Suzuki while Bob had been sidelined. Trash talk developed between the two, and it sort of came to a head at Saddleback. In the first moto, Bob felt that Kent was making a jerk out of him because it seemed Howerton was toying with Hannah instead of racing. Anyway, Bob got pissed and T-boned the Rhinestone Cowboy in a corner. When Howerton got up, Bob let him by to win the first moto. The second moto, Bob won fair and square and won the overall. Howerton was not a happy camper.

In the end Bob just couldn't overcome the problems we had with the bike and 1981 went down as a bad season.

It took time for Hannah to recover from his 1979 broken leg. He spent all of 1980 in rehab and trying to get into shape, but by the 1981 Mid-Ohio Trans-AMA, the Hurricane was back in form. *Werner Straub; Terry Good*

In 1981, after recovering from a badly broken leg, Bob Hannah resumed racing on Team Yamaha. At an Outdoor National event held at Saddleback Park in California, Hannah had an untimely disagreement with fellow competitor Kent Howerton and, after several bumping incidents, Hannah took off like a man possessed, leaving Howerton behind. This sequence shows Hannah riding flat out over obstacles like the infamous "Magoo Double" jump *(above left). Terry Good*

In 1982, Yamaha team manager Kenny Clark decided that Broc Glover would go to the 250cc class in the Nationals and Bob Hannah would ride 125cc. This situation did not sit well with Bob. My own personal opinion is that Bob felt that Yamaha was not stepping up to the plate for him when it came to bike development and, at the time, Honda had a huge program. It crossed his mind that if he stayed with Yamaha he would be struggling, and if he would go to Honda there was a chance to extend his career and make some money. So he went to Honda in 1983.

I know Bob might feel like I'm full of crap, but there were other things going on in his personal life that affected his move to Honda and his general feeling about racing. And, I think that some of his decisions were influenced by his accident.

You know the movie *Rocky,* when Rocky Balboa comes out of nowhere and boxing becomes his life, and because of that he won? Well, that had been Bob. He came out of a trailer in the desert eating avocadoes and peanut butter. Racing was his life, he was totally dedicated every minute of every day. Bob raced for his living. And, even when he was winning, everything and his riding was magic; he didn't enjoy the fruits of life. He was regimented and dedicated to winning. Nothing else mattered.

But when he got hurt, he had a lot of time on his hands and he started thinking. He developed a passion for flying, and that sort of took over as a major part of his interests. Suddenly we were spending less time talking about the bike and less time together practicing. Instead of traveling together in the race van, Bob would fly his plane. My description was that he began to get humanized. He saw the world, and he enjoyed what he saw. Don't get me wrong. He never lost his drive and determination to race; it was just that other things cropped into the picture.

We actually talked about me going with him to Honda, but I never really wanted to leave Yamaha. Our glory days were over, and there comes a time when you do what is best for your own future.

For me, the greatest thing about our years as a team was Bob's passion for winning and his determination to make it happen. Second on the list was the fun we had off-track. Bob's sense of humor and his small circle of friends kept the rigors of traveling enjoyable. We won our share of championships and had our time of controversy, but overall the fans loved the Hurricane and at places like Unadilla (his favorite track) they treated him like a rock star. Bob always showed a contentious exterior at the races. The fans loved him and many of the riders disliked him, but he always put on a show. We have remained friends to this day and that is what is most important in my story.

Good buddy and solid member of the Hannah inner circle is ex-factory rider Jeff Hicks. Jeff helped tell the Hannah story and was witness to his Honda and Suzuki years. *TMP*

As dedicated as he was to motocross racing, that same fiery spirit transcended into his love for flying. Now an airplane dealer, Hannah loves flying. Shown here is his high-performance Pitts Aerobatic craft. Note Ashley the Wonder Dog at rest. *TMP*

STAND ME UP! JUST STAND ME UP!

Originally from Atwater, Ohio, Jeff Hicks found his way to California as a privateer professional motocross rider. He built a reputation as a tough competitor and competed in both the AMA National Outdoor Championship series and the Supercross series riding an assortment of motorcycles, including Yamaha, KTM, Honda, and Suzuki. Hicks witnessed firsthand some of the most difficult times in Bob Hannah's career. He offers a unique perspective to the story; he saw things through the eyes of a competitor and professional rider. Jeff, now retired from racing, owns a construction company in Idaho. His insight is valuable to understanding the total picture of the Hurricane.

Bob and his buddies Greg Vonlossberg (kneeling in front) and Jeff Hicks on Lake Mead. During breaks between Supercross and Outdoor National seasons, Bob would rent a large houseboat for a week and invite his friends down to relax and do some water skiing. *Hannah*

In late 1980, at the Mid-Ohio Trans-AMA, Bob made his return to active competition after breaking his leg in a water-skiing accident. *Werner Straub; Terry Good*

JEFF HICKS

In 1981, I had quit my job at a motorcycle shop in Ohio and decided to come west. I wanted to run the full 1982 season, and that meant coming to California.

I signed a support deal with Yamaha in December of 1981, and was looking for a riding-apparel sponsor. Someone told me to call Hannah Racing Products and so I did, and Bob answered the phone. Bob told me that he had gotten wind of my deal with Yamaha and wanted to know who my mechanic was. I told him I didn't know yet and he quickly recommended Bevo. That didn't work out, but I did eventually get the riding gear deal with Hannah Racing Products.

As the 1982 season started, I got the idea that Bob was not comfortable hanging out with his teammates. There was a lot of pressure going on around the Yamaha team, and the young riders like Mike Bell, Rick Johnson, and Broc Glover wanted to make their own mark in the sport and they didn't want to play second fiddle to Hannah. Bob told me that he rode with some of his personal friends and, if I needed someplace to practice, I was welcome to come with him to the desert.

Bob had come back 100 percent from his broken leg and had made 1981 his comeback year. In '82 there were some differences in the factory bike design, and Bob and his mechanic, Keith McCarty, decided they preferred to test and practice on their own. In reality, they were trying to get the bike to work and fit Bob's riding style. I ended up spending a lot of time riding with Bob and Keith during that '82 season.

At the end of 1982, Yamaha did not renew my contract because my results had not been up to their expectations. At the same time, Bob was having his own issues with Yamaha.

The problems culminated in Bob leaving Yamaha for Honda.

I ended up with a deal from KTM to ride the Golden State series in California, and Bob was getting ready to start his contract with Honda. He asked me if I wanted to continue to train with him and I agreed. From day one, Hannah was on a mission to prove to Yamaha they had made a huge mistake in letting him move to Honda. He started training harder than I'd ever seen him train before. His mechanic was Brian Lunniss, and they would test his new Honda every day. Bob rode forty days straight at one point without so much as a half day off. A typical day began at sun up; we would ride bicycles over a set course at a pace faster than I thought could be done. Breakfast, then test riding two motos, debriefs with Brian, and then Bob would head home. Before dinner he would go for a run, do weight training, then in bed. He put himself on a strict schedule, no time for anything but training, testing, and more training.

I began to learn from him. I got tougher and in better shape than I thought possible. I actually started to ride better, more consistent, and less fatigue. Bob never coached me. That is just not his style, and he was too focused on his own program. But, every once in a while he would offer a quick remark: do this or do that, maybe use the front brake more aggressively. I just watched and absorbed as much as I could.

Along with an education in riding, I also got some insight into the politics of being a factory rider. There was never any letting up or taking it easy. It all began to pay off for me. My riding got better and I won more money and it certainly extended my career by two or three years.

Before the end of the Golden State series, I had a bad crash; broke my nose, loosened up some teeth, and cut my face. Hannah said the bikes I was riding were junk and he told me that he could get Honda to make me part of their support program. He was winning races and had some power with Honda, so it happened and I got on the program.

I used up four bikes by the end of the season, and I found out later that Bob had actually bought a couple of the bikes from Honda just so I could stay current. When Honda realized how serious Bob took my riding career, they agreed to supply me with better equipment and, although I never signed an official contract, I was getting great equipment.

In 1983, Bob started the season strong. He was leading the Supercross series and the National series. About two thirds through the season, there was a night indoor race at Orlando, Florida. Bob's friend John Savitski had gone from racing motocross to building tracks, and he needed a rider to do a light test for the track. The advantage of doing the test a night before the event was to get a bunch of practice laps in with nobody watching. Bob wanted to take advantage of every opportunity to beat the others, so he said yes and invited me along. We got there and it was just us two riding, Bob's mechanic, Brian Lunniss, was pumped at the chance of dialing in the track. We hadn't ridden one lap when Bob does a huge loop off a double jump, hits the ground, and breaks his wrist.

The season went downhill from there. David Bailey, Bob's teammate, was hot and riding hard. He ended up winning the Supercross series and the 250cc National series.

Hannah tried to come back but he had to use a brace and tape his wrist, and that didn't work. So, basically, 1983 was junk. Bob decided to take a month off and heal; he was also putting together a deal to go to Italy and ride a few non-championship races.

After a month of rehab, we go out to Tehachapi, in the desert, for some practice. Lunniss brings a couple of works bikes and a few of Bob's regular desert riding cronies show up to ride with us. Everybody is warming up their bikes. I'm getting my gear on inside of my van. Just as I'm about to fire my bike I hear somebody yelling, "Bob went down, and he's hurt." We all start heading for where he crashed, about one hundred yards from our camp. Bob is laying face down in a twenty-five-foot deep wash. He had gone over the bars, and the bike had speared him. It didn't take a doctor to figure out that he was really hurt.

Actually, by the time I got there, the guys had gotten the bike off of him and he was yelling, "Stand me

A worried-looking Brian Lunniss watches practice at the 1983 Anaheim, California, Supercross. This was the first year Lunniss and Hannah were teamed together. The match was good for all concerned. *TMP*

The Hurricane gets ready for battle at the Seattle Kingdome in 1983. Bob could have won the Supercross title except he broke his wrist and never really recovered, riding hurt the remainder of the season. *TMP*

up! Just stand me up!" Hannah was very concerned about having his back broken and being paralyzed. It was a fear we all had. Nobody wants to crash and then ride a wheelchair for the rest of their life.

When they stood him up, he was shaking and quivering in pain and shock. Sweat was pouring off of his face and the front of his white riding pants were stained with a huge spot of blood. It looked like he had been shot.

We had to carry him back to the camp. It was before cell phones. There was no way we could get a sheriff helicopter or paramedic chopper out there, so the guys loaded him into my van and I had to drive him to Lancaster [California] hospital. It took about forty minutes to an hour to get to the hospital. Bob thought he was going to die; shock set in and he was in really bad shape.

Once the doctors began treatment and Brian and several of the others showed up. Bob realized that he wasn't going to die, and things got a little calmer.

It was determined that when the bike hit Bob from the back, the impact spread his hips apart, broke his pelvis, and crushed his bladder. The injuries were much more serious than anyone ever knew, and there were questions as to whether or not he would ever ride again. The press found out about the crash and treated it just like they did when he broke his leg. But, in reality, they never knew how bad things got.

After the pelvis injury, the years of pounding his body started to build up. He still had his drive and his desire to win, but now he had to push himself even harder to stay in shape. I was racing in Europe at the end of '83, so I missed most of his comeback training, but I know how tough it was for him.

The Hurricane gets some air under his wings at the 1985 AMA 250cc Outdoor National at Hangtown, California. *TMP*

At the end of 1983, Bob's contract with Honda was over, so he had to convince them that he was still good enough to win in '84. He'd have to tell you the story, but I guess he ditched the crutches in the parking lot the day he went in for contract talks. By the time he came back out of the building, he was signed for 1984 and 1985. No one was better at contract negotiations than Hannah.

He was true to his word and won some races in 1984, but again struggled with injuries. I think he came back way too soon from the pelvis injury. O'Mara won the Supercross title for Honda, and Rick Johnson on a Yamaha won the 250cc National title.

In the '85 Supercross season, the San Diego Supercross was a bummer for Hannah. For the first time in his career, he failed to qualify for a main event. He never said anything to me at the time, but I knew he was pissed. I knew it was a culmination of several things, starting with his one wrecked ankle, which he was unable to set down on a hard-packed, concrete-like track—typical of the San Diego SX. On top of that, he was still having trouble with his wrist and his previous pelvis injury, and they all blew up in his face that night. What do you do? But it didn't matter what the circumstances were, he hated to do that in front of his fans. I know it bothered him.

He managed to overcome that night and went on riding hard and coming back as "Hurricane II" and still was able to win races. There is one thing about Hannah's personality that never changes: he deals with problems in his own private way. He doesn't share with the outside world. No matter the situation, he deals with it and moves on.

During the 1985 Outdoor National series, Hannah was riding extremely well, but injuries prevented him from taking the title. He remarked during an interview for this book that during his Honda years he was riding better than he had ever ridden. *TMP*

Getting ready for battle, Bob Hannah locks in his concentration as he waits for the start of the 1986 Supercross at the Los Angeles Coliseum. In all his years of racing, the Los Angeles Supercross was never kind to the Hurricane. *TMP*

In 1986, Bob went to Suzuki and signed to a development program and rode selected Supercross and National events. The funny thing about that deal was the fact that some of the same people who had let him go in 1975 were still there. Now they wanted him back.

At first the bikes were not very good, but Bob seemed to be re-energized and ready to give his best in developing the program.

After he had worked a couple months on the program, I joined the test team to help sort out the problems with the bike. As the program progressed, it was obvious that I was struggling on the bike and Bob was getting very aggravated about not getting Suzuki improve their suspension system at a faster pace.

We went down to the Suzuki test track near San Diego to go testing. Bob had a factory works bike and I was on a modified production bike. A couple of laps into the session, my bike pops into neutral and I do a huge endo and get hit with the rear suspension and it takes a giant chunk of meat out of my butt. A short time later, the same thing happens to Bob and he does an endo, breaking his collarbone. We had to take him to the hospital. He was pissed. It could have been another pelvis or a leg or even a broken back. He didn't have to say a word, but you knew that he was torn apart about getting hurt again. But, Hannah being Hannah, eight weeks later he was back testing, and they finally started getting things sorted out. Bob helped Eyvind Boyesen develop what they called the Boyesen-link system and he used that system to win the USGP at Unadilla that year. It was a momentous boost to his career and his fans went nuts.

Things were up and down for the rest of 1986. Bob failed to qualify at the Los Angeles Coliseum Supercross, and the press made a big deal out of it.

He came back in 1987 and won the Motocross des Nations and continued with Suzuki for a number of years, riding and doing PR. I rode Honda from that point on and we didn't race together much.

In the late 1970s, Bob bought this rustic home in Ketchum, Idaho, located a short distance from the famed Hemingway Estate. Later, Hannah moved to his ranch in Caldwell, Idaho. *TMP*

WHEAT

HANNAH
43
WHEAT

HANNAH
43
WHEAT

Opposite: Hannah ran a test session for the engineers on the 1987 Suzuki. Photographers, anxious to get a good photo, instead got a lesson in how to take dirty pictures. *TMP*

Hannah has had a great impact on my life, and we've remained best friends long after the two of us retired from professional motocross racing. I'm sure he extended my motocross career by at least a few years. After racing, I started my own home-construction business in Idaho, and when I got a little tight on funds in the beginning Bob was a great friend there as well. He propped up my business a few times to keep it going. It's impossible to be around him and not be influenced by his drive and determination. He never looks at the bad side of things. Today, we enjoy life and spend time flying, hunting, drinking sweet tea, and getting out on our Harleys. Oh yeah...and petting golden retrievers.

YOU GOT MY MONEY?

In the time before instant text messaging and jumbo outdoor TV screens, the only way fans could understand who was doing what on a racetrack was to depend on the track announcer. As a matter of fact, the announcer played a dramatic role in events. When the Supercross series came to enclosed stadiums, colorful figures like Larry "Supermouth" Huffman made the races more exciting by whipping the fans into hysteria as the riders fought for positions on the track.

Another of only a few track announcers who won national attention for his fervor, and a man who became instrumental in building the mystique of the Hurricane, was Larry Maiers. Larry was there during the glory years and became one of Hannah's closest friends. Now living near Atlanta, Maiers relived some of the more interesting times spent with the Hurricane.

Longtime buddy and noted track announcer Larry Maiers does an interview with the Hurricane. According to Larry, he had to keep a tight rein on Hannah to prevent some R-rated remarks. The two friends were well-known for playing mean tricks on each other. *Larry Maiers*

LARRY MAIERS

At the time I met Bob Hannah, I was working for John Penton Motorcycles. Penton imported motorcycles, along with a line of accessories. The top product in the Penton accessory line was Hi-Point riding boots. In the old days, riders would use lumberjack boots or telephone lineman boots, so when a specialty boot like the Hi-Point came to market, they were by far the most popular with riders. Bob had been buying Hi-Point boots since he started racing but, frankly, I had never heard of Bob Hannah until he showed up at the Florida winter series in the late '70s. Bob was in the lead for the Open Championship, and Hi-Point had a contingency program for wearing their boots. When you won races or a championship, we paid.

The promoter, who was a friend of mine, took me over to meet Hannah. It was obvious that he was about to win the championship and the promoter figured we should meet. I greeted Bob and the first words out of his mouth were, "You got my money?"

Three old buddies ham it up for the TV cameras during an interview at Bob Hannah's last race at Unadilla in New York. Larry Maiers (left), Gary Bailey (middle), and Hannah (right) have been close friends for decades. *Gary Bailey*

There was no "Hello. How are you?" No "Nice to meet you." Nothing! Just "You got my money?"

I told him, "No, I don't have any money; I'll have to send it to you."

He said, "When?"

By this time I was pissed and thinking what a jerk this guy is. Anyway, he kept it up and after he won the first moto of the event, he came over and wanted to know if I got his money yet.

He won the championship that day, so I went over to congratulate him and I told him, "You won so we owe you so much money and I'll mail it to you as soon as I get back to the shop." He said, "Oh gee, I wish you would have brought a check with you."

Now I was mad, so I asked him, "What the hell is your problem?" He said, "Well, I'm new at this, and I'm told that some of you guys skip out on paying." I was so mad that I went over to the promoter, Bill West, and borrowed the money we owed Hannah and took it over and said, "Here's your f***ing money."

Years later, Hannah told me, "It was my mechanic, Bill Buchka, who told me to be careful because sometimes you don't get paid. I didn't know any better."

Our first meeting was just about our last.

Time passed, and I got into the announcing gig through a friend of mine who promoted races at Red Bud in Michigan. It happened that his regular announcer didn't show for a race and he asked me if I could call it.

Back in those days, there was never any money for promotion, so with Hi-Point paying me to go to the races, it became an added dimension if I could announce the race and promote Hi-Point boots at the same time. Most promoters were happy to trade a name title for an event in exchange for a free announcer.

I started paying attention to other announcers like Larry Huffman, Dave Despain, and Bruce Flanders. Over time I got better and then, because there were only a few announcers doing motocross, I started getting paid.

I ended up doing the Nationals, Supercross, and AMA Flat Track races in the east. In California, Mike Goodwin and Larry Huffman struck a deal, so I only did a few races out west. Goodwin would work Huffman and I against each other by telling one of us the other was working for less money.

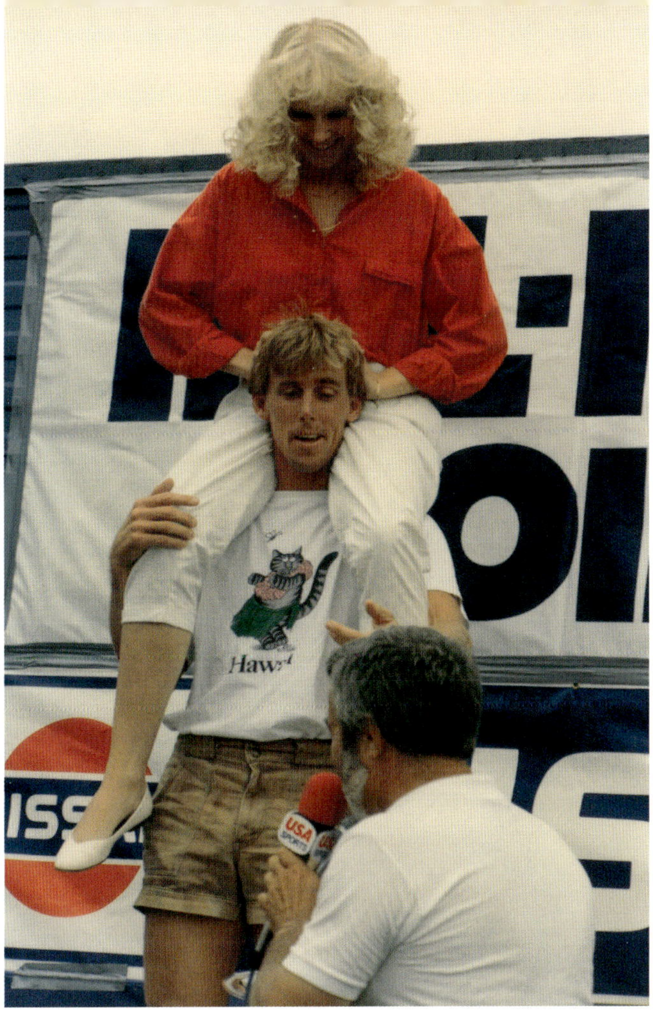

Track announcer Larry Maiers tries to control the Hurricane during interviews at Unadilla in 1986 and 1987, a couple of years before Hannah retired at the very same track. In 1987 Bob is wearing a yellow T-shirt and an unusual hat. The other shots are from 1986. *Larry Maiers*

Finally, I gave up announcing from the booth and began doing color commentating from the floor of the major stadiums. I got to know all of the stars and everything about their careers. My specialty became interviews before, during, and after the races.

Actually, I had two careers going on at the same time. I never stopped my relationship with Hi-Point and the promotion of their boots and riding gear. We developed a payout system for any rider winning a major event wearing Hi-Point boots. It got crazy because the riders were all looking for a few extra bucks. There was a time when forty riders would line up at a Supercross main event, and all forty had Hi-Point boots. In Hannah's case, all anyone had to do was put money on the line and he was going for it. Bob became our best promotion.

Known for years as "Buckwheat" to his friends, Hannah changed his logo to "Wheat" in 1987 when he was riding for Suzuki. The reason remains unknown, but some speculate it was rooted in political correctness. *TMP*

My opinion about Hannah began to soften after I took a tour of the Yamaha racing department with Bob, his mechanic, Keith McCarty, and Yamaha rider John Savitsky. After that tour, I would find myself hanging out with McCarty, Bob, and Bevo at the races, and we all became friends.

This was the time of Hannah's glory days, and it was his notoriety and popularity with fans that made the races so exciting to call. The biggest attraction to Bob held by his fans, aside from the fact that he was winning, came from his never-give-up attitude. The fans loved that about him. I remember one time he fell about four or five times during a moto, but he kept getting up and finally won the race. The other aspect about Hannah that drew fans to him was the fact that he would never say anything in the press to appease

Even late in his career, on any day Hannah could smoke the competition. He always claimed other riders were smoother but, to his fans, the Hurricane had his own special style. *TMP*

anyone. He always said what he was thinking, which meant that in some cases his comments were not politically correct. To the journalists covering motorcycle racing, his straight up remarks would piss some people off. Many magazine writers thought of Bob Hannah as an arrogant, self-centered wise mouth, and what made things worse was the fact that he didn't give a crap.

The fans picked up on this and liked it. Hannah was a working-class guy who fought hard and didn't take any crap from the establishment. His job, he felt, was to win races, beat the other riders, and not really to make friends.

It was obvious to me and everyone who showed up at the racetrack who was popular. After the races, it didn't matter where he finished, the line around

Hannah's trailer was the biggest. Sure, the other name riders would have fans around, but nothing like the crowds Bob produced. He played to the audience. Standing in the back of his race hauler, Bob would talk and joke with the crowd. He would usually steal the trophy girl or flirt with the tight bodies hanging around. The fans would go nuts; guys would just laugh when their girl friends chanted "Hannah" or screamed for him to toss his riding shirt into the mob. Bob would sign autographs until everyone who wanted a signature got one.

Hannah's wild riding style also created an opportunity for race fans to rally around him. It was common, at the Nationals and Supercross events, for Hannah to get tangled up in the pack on the first lap. As the field strung out, Hannah would start picking off riders one at a time. And with every pass, the fan roar would grow just a little louder. Because he was providing a lot of the action, it was easy for announcers, like me, to pick up on his charge to the front and start whipping the crowd. Larry Huffman was famous for screaming "Here comes Hannah" during the stadium races. Imagine 40,000 fans; toss in a few beers and you could create a real scene.

BOB "HURRICANE" HANNAH, 1976 125cc NATIONAL CHAMPION

The Hurricane struck hard in his very first year as a professional rider. In 1976, Hannah exploded onto the American motocross scene by taking the AMA 125cc Outdoor National title away from then golden-boy Marty Smith of Team Honda. *Yamaha PR*

At the Outdoor Nationals it was the same thing. Fans around the track depended on the announcer to let them know what was happening. I would work hard to keep them informed and when Bob was coming to the front, you could really get the crowd rocking.

At Red Bud, the announcing booth was located on a hill in the center of the track. People couldn't see around either side of the track so, on this particular day, Hannah starts hauling to the front and I start barking in the microphone to keep everyone informed when, suddenly, the crowd begins running from one side of the track to the other side every lap. Fans were jumping over the fences and waving Hannah to go faster. It was a wild situation and the crazier the fans got, the better he liked it.

Bob's riding philosophy was "ride hard and fast but not dirty." However, if he caught some backmarker and let him know he was behind, then Bob figured that rider should move over. If the rider didn't move, Hannah would pass anyway. If it meant knocking the rider down, so be it.

Say what you will about today's hero riders, but at the pinnacle of his career—'77, '78, '79—it didn't matter what track, indoor or outdoor, the majority of the fans loved Hannah.

I remember two places in particular during the Supercross series—Seattle and the Pontiac Silverdome in Michigan—where Bob would bring the house down. I think the Silverdome was where some fan brought out hurricane warning flags and put them up in the stands. It was amazing to witness.

Don't get me wrong. Bob Hannah was not the first American motocross hero. Going back a few years there was Gary Bailey, Jimmy Weinert, Jim Pomeroy, and Brad

YAMAHA
When you know how they're built.

Team Yamaha's Bob "Hurricane" Hannah, 1978 American Motorcyclist Association's Professional Athlete of the Year, and the "winningest" rider in the United States motor sports history, is the heavy favorite to successfully defend his triple championship reign.

The Supercross held in the Detroit Silverdome was one of Hannah's favorite events. The crowds loved him, and he managed win the two-day event several times. Hannah was king of all motocross during the 1978 and 1979 seasons. *Yamaha PR; Dennis Kanegae*

The end of a colorful career took place in July of 1989. At his favorite track, Unadilla, New York, and surrounded by his fans, Hannah said goodbye to a brilliant career. Longtime buddy Larry Maiers did the final interview. *Larry Maiers*

Lackey. Then, as the sport grew in popularity, Marty Smith took the title as motocross hero. Marty was good-looking, fast, soft spoken, polite, and a truly likable person. No one ever accused Bob Hannah of being nice. When Hannah hit the motocross bigtime, he was fast, wild, outspoken, determined, and mean. He didn't just win races, he punished the field. The fans loved his attitude.

In my opinion, although Hannah was spectacular in Supercross, his real love for riding a motorcycle came with the outdoor season and the national championship. And, of all the tracks used for that series, again in my opinion, none was more suited to his personality than Unadilla at Binghamton, New York. Some of the magazine writers called Unadilla the "Woodstock" of motocross. In Hannah's day it had all the ingredients: wild fans, hot weather, an all-natural track, beer, half-naked girls, and the "Hill People." Nowhere on earth could be more suited to the Hurricane style.

Bob loved the place because it was so damn rough. It was only used once a year, so it was left natural until the race. Nobody touched it. It would still be covered with pasture grass on the first day of practice. It had rocks and holes and ruts. There were ever-changing lines, and if you lost concentration for an instant, you were eating dirt. It was a kidney cracking, ankle breaking, blister rising, and arm pumping plot of dirt waiting to kick your ass in a heartbeat. Bob embraced the challenge, knowing that riders who didn't grow up riding rough terrain would hate it. The fans went nuts for Hannah; they brought signs, chanted his name, and cursed his rivals. He retired there. He was part of the American Motocross des Nations team [Rick Johnson, Hannah, and Jeff Ward], winning his class on a 125cc Suzuki. He beat the O'Show [Johnny O'Mara] after Johnny ran out of gas with one lap to go. Always truthful, Hannah told the crowd that he didn't deserve to win, that Johnny had beat him fair and square but just ran out of gas.

When TV picked up on motocross racing, I had a show called *MotoWorld* on the USA Network and, later, on ESPN. I had Bob come on as a guest in studio, and also as a color commentator at the races. After he retired, Bob and I stayed friends, but our careers moved in different directions.

Looking back over the years, there is one thing that always struck me as to why Hannah was different than other professional riders. I learned early on that when he would come into a city to race, he never stayed in fancy hotels like many of the riders. He had friends all over the country, not racers, just friends, and he would stay with them. He loved staying with regular folks and he enjoyed home cooking. He told me many times about staying with author Tom Madigan and his wife, Darlene, and sitting down to Big D's fried chicken, mashed potatoes, green beans, and homemade biscuits. Then, after stuffing himself to the breaking point, he would demand a large helping of Darlene's famous banana cream pie. He trusted the people he called friends and, although they came from all walks of life, he never played favorites. Everyone was treated equal. He always paid back any kindness shown to him.

In his private life, Bob Hannah has never been one for the congestion of the city. As soon as he could afford the move, he made his way to the wilds of Idaho, which allowed him to hunt, fish, and train. Airplanes are also a big part of his life in Idaho; note the license plate (Pitts Special, his aerobatic airplane). *TMP*

HANNAH
7
HANNAH
Silkolene

His loyalty carried over from friends to the companies he called sponsors. For example: At one point in his career, Scott USA came up with an all-plastic riding boot that would hold a rider's ankle in place without flex. The boots were solid plastic from the foot to near the knee with only a hinge action to allow movement of the foot. Hannah came up to me and said, "Look, I've tried these boots on and I really don't like them, but there is a chance that this boot can keep my ankles from further damage. But Hi-Point has been so good to me that if you say no, I won't use them. I'll live up to my contract."

We never had a signed contract with Bob Hannah, only word of mouth and a handshake. I told him if wearing Scott boots is going to be safer and help prolong his career, just do it. His health was more important than a few advertising bucks. Later, he came back to Hi-Point.

Because I had announced so many motocross races over the years, people constantly ask me, who is the best rider in motocross? The reality to that question is there can't be a reasonable answer. There is no way to compare. If you ask Bob who is best he will tell you he thinks Ricky Carmichael or Jeremy McGrath are great. James Stewart is going to be a record breaker. So, there is no way to compare. My feeling is that after Hannah retired, the bike technology went through the roof. And the riders developed training programs, with personal trainers, new diets, weight training; today the riders have programs similar to world class Olympic contestants. Hannah, Roger DeCoster, Pierre Karsmakers, and Heikki Mikkola never had any programs other than their own determination.

I also feel that Carmichael and McGrath were able to intimidate riders just by coming to the starting line. In Hannah's time, the riders would never let anyone intimidate them. They would train and race hard and at least let you know they were there. I mean, there is no way DeCoster, Rick Johnson, Kent Howerton, Jimmy Weinert, or Mike Bell would worry about racing Bob Hannah. On the track, they all hated him. Even his good buddy, Marty Tripes, would kick his ass if he had the chance.

It boils down to the fact that you can't compare [riders from different eras]. But in his time, Bob Hannah was the best. He never gave up, and that is what earned him the respect of the fans.

In closing, my personal Hannah story is very simple, but shows his real human side. After his retirement, I came up to his ranch in Idaho for a visit. It just happened that we were looking at his gun collection, and two guns in particular caught my eye. Hannah is not only an avid hunter, but one of his heroes has always been [the late] John Wayne. As part of his retirement, Suzuki invited John Wayne's son, Ethan, to present Bob with a John Wayne Winchester Commemorative rifle. I commented, "Wow, if I could afford it, I would love one of those guns just to hang on the wall." Unknown to me, Bob had actually bought one of those guns as a match to the one he had been given. He looked at me and said, "You don't have to buy one, I want you to have one of mine." He gave me one of those guns.

CASTING A BIG SHADOW

Anyone even remotely connected to a factory motocross team during the 1970s and 1980s knows the name Bevo. His real name (or taxable name as he puts it) is Robert Forti (misspelled Forte by the press for years), but "Bevo" works just fine. A one-time team mechanic and, later, a factory representative for Scott USA, Bevo was a major player at all of the major National and Supercross events during Bob Hannah's entire career. Robust in size, Bevo offered his opinion on all subjects related to motocross, including the riders, motorcycles, rules and regulations, the fans, and the sport in general. Aside from offering opinions, Bevo was usually the center of any and all fun, mischief, misconduct, or controversy found in the pits.

Hannah once said, "Bevo was one of the few people who would tell me straight out what he thought. If I was riding like an old woman, and won a race, Bevo would tell me I rode like an old woman."

Bevo and Hannah became friends during their time at Yamaha and have remained such through the years. No story of the Hurricane's fame would be complete without a few comments from Bevo.

Opposite: Always candid, Hannah would speak his mind when asked a question. If the answer was not what the interviewer wanted to hear, it was too bad. Shown here is Hannah giving the crowd a few words at the 1986 Los Angeles Coliseum Supercross. *TMP*

BEVO

I met Hannah the first year he came to the Florida series with Keith McCarty. We were all wondering who the kid was who seemed to be setting the world on fire. He was all over the motorcycle and his riding style was something none of us had ever seen. Actually, Bob had won the 1976 National 125cc Championship with Bill Buchka as his mechanic, but then Buchka left and McCarty took over as nursemaid. We all figured here was a one-year wonder.

Hannah won the first race of the series and we all said, "He was lucky to get out of the first week alive; he will never make it the second week the way he rode."

He won the second week and just kept on winning. At the time, I was a factory mechanic for Yamaha and my rider was Donnie Cantaloupi. However, I developed a good friendship with Keith McCarty and ended up hanging out with him, Hannah, and a young rider named John Savitski. Hannah had taken John under his wing and helped him get a Yamaha support ride offered to privateers.

Riders being riders, we had some issues with Hannah and Cantaloupi when they would bang together during a race, but I never confronted Bob; I just let the riders work things out. Bob was very aggressive and he had what he called "Hannah Law," which meant that if you got in his way, he moved you out, and if you didn't like it, tough.

During the period of 1977 to 1979, Bob was at his career pinnacle and it was very exciting to watch him race. He was not known for his holeshot starts, so he would usually end up in the rear of the pack on lap one and have to cut through traffic to win. Larry "Supermouth" Huffman was famous for whipping the fans into a frenzy by asking, "Where's Hannah?" Suddenly the crowd would go nuts trying to find the Hurricane. He won a lot of races from the back of the pack. It was amazing, because you could never count him out until the checker flag flew.

The Hurricane won all of his championships on Yamahas. His titles included the 1976 125cc National Championship, 1977 250cc Supercross Championship, 1978 250cc National and Supercross Championships, 1978 Trans-AMA Championship, and the 1979 250cc National and Supercross Championships. *Dennis Kanegae*

In time, a small group—Keith, Larry Maiers, Hannah, Marty Tripes, and Savitski—seemed to end up hanging out together. There was always plenty of fun, jokes, and other stuff to break up the boredom that comes with being on the road.

There are so many stories about Hannah's career that it is impossible to remember everything, but there are a few nuggets I can share. The first one that comes to mind is early in Bob's career. He went to Europe to ride in the Motocross des Nations and the Trophée des Nations events. I was a privateer mechanic at the time, and McCarty got me a ticket to work with Team Yamaha. If I remember correctly, one of the races was in Germany and the other in Belgium. Anyway, Hannah has always stayed in his own little world at the races and never paid much attention to anything but his job as a rider. Bob rode a 500cc in Germany, and he went out for the first moto oblivious to all the other riders. During the race he rode hard and battled handlebar to handlebar with this other Yamaha rider. After the moto, Bob came storming in and said, "Who was that joker who was racing me so hard? I should be able to beat anybody on a Yamaha, what's the deal?" Come to find out the other rider was World Champion Heikki Mikkola. Bob hadn't even paid attention to who was in the lineup at the starting gate.

After Bob came back from his broken leg, Yamaha put him on a 125cc during the 1982 season. At first he didn't like it at all, but Yamaha paid him a bonus. Contrary to all the stories, Yamaha never doubted his ability or didn't try to test him. But the motorcycle industry was in a funk and Yamaha decided to cut back

Bevo Forti will always be one of the most beloved personalities in motocross. Here he is in his typical racetrack garb. *Hannah*

SMITH
DUNLOP
SMITH
DUNLOP
TIRES
SMITH
12
12

on their race team efforts. I had been reallocated from team mechanic to being in charge of the parts truck that the factory sent to the races. Then, Bob and Yamaha had some type of falling out and, in 1983, he went to Honda and Yamaha decided to discontinue my job. Hannah had always acted as a kind of shield at Yamaha when it came to my position and, with him gone, I had lost my protection. I took a trip to Sun Valley, Idaho, Hannah's home at the time, and ended up getting a job with Scott USA as a field representative. I also worked with Bob on his motocross schools doing all the mechanical work on his bikes.

As Hannah's career went on, his injuries and some bike problems caused him to lose some of the dominance he once had. The more difficult things got, the more he worked. His personality began to turn inside him. The irony with Bob was that he didn't want to just win; he wanted to beat the competition into the ground. When he walked through the pit area, he wanted the other riders to look away. No matter how much of a points lead he had in a series, he would still practice every day, ride in the mud and bad weather. He would train and ride; he just wouldn't stop.

For example, he had an eighty-point lead when he did the so-called "light check" down in Orlando and crashed, breaking his wrist. He didn't have to do that. It was like he was possessed. My feeling is that he just wore himself out. Once he decided he couldn't do it anymore, it was tough for him to accept. Hannah once told me, "You know, it takes big balls to do a triple jump, and mine have been busted so many times they won't hold air."

What Bob didn't understand was that the fans still loved him. He would get down on himself and I would tell him, "Hey man, even when you're running sixteenth, the fans are all screaming for you." Hannah was the first U.S. rider to dominate the way he did. Bob pioneered training, and worked harder than anyone he rode against. He was ruthless and never gave up; fans liked that. When Hannah was on top, you have to remember that the motocross industry was still in its infancy, and the factory bikes were not always the greatest. Hannah gave the fans what they paid money to see. He would start in the back of the pack and then come flying over the jumps all out of control. He did whatever it took to win; no style points. In fact Hannah hated his style. In his eyes, Marty Tripes was a rider with class and style.

Because Hannah didn't pose for the press, he got a lot of bad ink. The magazines would say he was not a good spokesman for the sport and he was mean spirited. The truth was, on the track he didn't want any friends. And he would cover his emotions with a tough-guy image so the competition could never find a weakness.

Off the track and away from the media, Hannah was a totally different person. His small circle of friends was lucky to see that part of his character. Off-track and on the road, Hannah was notorious for having fun, playing jokes, and enjoying life.

Because of my size, I was never one of Bob's training buddies. I was his eating buddy. On the road, Hannah's schedule was over the top; just training and riding every day, in bed by eight and up at the crack of dawn. However, after the races, win or lose, Sunday we would find a 7/11 and load up on junk food of every description and pig out.

Another one of Hannah's favorites was flying radio-controlled airplanes. One time we were staying at a Holiday Inn and Bob was flying a plane around the parking lot, doing tricks when he crashed it into this huge neon sign and punched a hole in it about two feet around, We had to avoid the hotel management until the races were over and we could clear out of town.

Track announcer Larry Maiers was one of Bob's prized targets when it came to playing jokes. One time we went fishing on this huge sport boat down in Florida. One of Bob's sponsors set it up. We fished all day and only caught this little foot-long sucker fish, so Hannah took it and stuffed it into Larry's motorhome, which was parked at the track. Four days later, Maiers showed up and couldn't figure out why it stunk.

Opposite: The team of Brian Lunniss and Bob Hannah worked extremely well together. Says Brian, "In 1983 we were leading the Supercross and the National Championship by mid-season. Bob was using the field for target practice. He was going to give Honda both titles. Then, in Orlando, he crashed and broke his wrist, and both Championships went down the toilet." *TMP*

Look closely at the riding style of the Hurricane during a 125cc Outdoor National at Saddleback Park in 1982. Every time the subject of riding style was brought up, Hannah would always say that riders like Bailey and O'Mara had style; he would simply hang on no matter what happened. *Larry Maiers*

Bob has always been a pyro, so another time he tossed this king-size M-80 under the same motorhome and it blew the water tank and part of the floor into the parking lot. Maiers came out with a .357 handgun, screaming at Hannah.

A lot of years have past since the Hurricane would strike fear in the heart of the racers who had to face him. Our lives have gone in different directions, but I was very lucky to have been a part of Hannah's career. If had to recall any single period in our friendship to best illustrate the Hannah personality, it would be the transition between his leaving Yamaha and joining Honda. He discontinued everything in his life—his airplane, hunting, fishing—except preparing to race. It was like a *Rocky* movie. He bought a heavy punching bag and would set up a timer and punch that bag for three-minute rounds

Hannah has always been known for telling things like they are, and the welcome sign to his ranch is no exception. Have a nice day. *TMP*

with the *Rocky* theme blasting out of a CD player. He'd go fifteen rounds, then weight lift until he was totally exhausted. Every day he went running first thing in the morning. His mechanic, Brian, would have bikes ready and the two of them would run at least two forty-minute motos, even if they had to drive a hundred miles to find good weather. During that period, I never saw anyone who wanted to win more than he did.

I think that he pushed himself so hard and raced so hard that he punished his body to a critical point. Looking back, it was the beginning of the final phase of his career. It is my belief that if Bob had not had the injuries, the year off, and the abuse to his body trying to stay competitive, he would have won many more races and several more championships. It would be hard to guess but I would stake a month's pay that he could have passed out a long list of ass-whippings before he finished his run.

For some unexplained reason, Hannah (right) and Bevo (left) dressed up as security officers and attacked their buddy, Larry Maiers. The story goes that the pair of phony cops took Maiers out of the motel only to cross paths with two real cops. *Larry Maiers*

Carrying the number one plate on his Yamaha, the Hurricane was a terror in the 250cc Outdoor National series in 1979. He won it and the Supercross Championship for the second straight year. *Dennis Kanegae*

5

HURRICANE WATCH: EYEWITNESS ACCOUNTS FROM A REPORTER ON THE SCENE

From the time I first met Bob Hannah in 1979 until the mid-1980s, I only managed to attend the occasional race. I was never witness to his glory days with Yamaha. As a journalist in business for myself, most of my assignments concentrated on automobile racing: dirt track, sports car, and drag racing were my main sources of income. This is not to say that Hannah was a stranger. On his West Coast tours during the Outdoor National series and the Supercross series, Bob would stay with my wife, Darlene, and me, using our home in Thousand Oaks as a base of operation. In turn, Darlene and I would vacation at his house in Idaho. In 1980, Hannah accompanied us to the Indy 500, but for the most part his racing career was distant from our lives.

Shortly after Bob signed with Honda in 1983, I got the idea of documenting some of the National and Supercross events with the plan of eventually producing a book. It was a great idea, but doomed to failure. In reality, traveling to the races worked out fine. Taking photos was no problem, the same with jotting down pages of notes during various events. But, when it came time to put the package together, the publisher had gone out of business and Hannah had decided he was not ready to devote the time necessary to relive his career. He was not retired.

On the contrary, he was under tremendous pressure from Honda to perform and was in the middle of a fierce battle for both the 250cc Outdoor National title and the Supercross crown. Complicating matters even further, he was fighting a rash of injuries that kept him in a state of constant pain. It was bad timing. Hannah was focused on riding, and when he is focused on (or, some might say, obsessed with) a subject, there is no deviation. Bad timing on my part, but I stayed with the project, always hoping for a change of heart. The materials I had gathered—the photos, notes, magazine articles, and press clippings—ended up lying dormant for over twenty years.

In 2007 I again approached Hannah about doing a book on his career. Long retired, I figured it was time. To my surprise, Hannah responded with as much enthusiasm as he felt necessary. "I don't care, if you want to do it, then do it." That was his way of saying yes.

As I said in the introduction, I devised a plan by which to tell the Bob Hannah story. I would challenge Hannah to offer his best memories of events he thought important. I would get word of mouth comments from a few of those close to Bob who had witnessed his career. Finally, I would break out my own personal notes taken during my observations of his career. The following are those notes, taken directly from accounts written at the time they happened (1983–1986) and delivered in a newswire-dateline type of format. Some of the accounts are colorful and extensive, while others are short and seemingly incomplete—such is the nature of note taking.

JANUARY 28, 1983, ANAHEIM, CALIFORNIA

Now on a Honda, with Brian Lunniss as mechanic, Hannah has been training like a man possessed and says he is ready. The rain-soaked supercross track inside Anaheim Stadium is very muddy. The biggest surprise of the evening comes early, when announcer Larry "Supermouth" Huffman introduces the riders. Huffman begins, "From Carson City, Nevada, the winningest rider in American motocross." That's as much as you can hear; the crowd begins cheering so loudly nothing else could be heard.

Bob is still recovering from a practice crash, and he seems to be in a great deal of pain as the evening progresses. Despite the pain, he wins the first heat race.

While getting the bike ready for the main event, Brian notices two Japanese guys using a very small camera to take pictures of the Honda. Turns out the guys are Yamaha engineers, and Lunniss chases them out of the pit.

Before the main, Hannah and Goat Breker (a fellow racer) talk candidly about recovering from recent injuries and how they are trying to get back into top shape. They also discuss the pressures placed on them by the factories while riding hurt.

During the feature, Hannah falls in turn one and has to come from the back of the pack to finish fourth. His teammate, David Bailey, wins the evening. It is a good start.

Above: A perfect shot of the Hurricane riding style, as Hannah launches off a jump at the 1984 Anaheim, California, Supercross. Bob often remarked that if he could have stayed injury-free during his Honda years, he would have won more championships. *TMP*

Right: Playing to an empty house; Bob Hannah concentrates on practice for the 1984 Anaheim Supercross. This was his first full season with Honda and he showed signs of the old Hurricane, but constant injuries hampered his career with the Red Bike team. *TMP*

FEBRUARY 12–13, 1983,
SEATTLE, WASHINGTON

Inside the Kingdome, track conditions are terrible—ruts, mud, and, as practice ends, the track is deteriorating rapidly. It is a two-day event. On Saturday night, Hannah wins going away. He also gets a rare holeshot in the main event. On Sunday, there is a huge crash at the start of the main, but Bob holds on to take the win. He is now tied with David Bailey for the points lead in the Supercross series. I notice that there may be some nervous tension at play during the Seattle race. Bob is very quiet and reserved, not talking much, and having many closed-door meetings with Brian. There was a mechanical issue during the Sunday race: the rear disc brake was locking up and Bob had to rely on the front brake only.

FEBRUARY 24, 1983,
EL TORO, CALIFORNIA

My wife, Darlene, and I are invited to attend a photo session for Bel-Ray Oil Company, one of Hannah's personal sponsors. We spend two days at Bob's house in Orange County. It is an extreme experience. I have never been exposed to the Hannah obsession and focus; most of my time spent with Bob off-track has been more casual. His training goes on no matter what other engagements he has, including the photo shoot. On the second afternoon, he goes running in a monsoon-like rain storm. When I ask him why, he replies, "Whenever I get tired, or the rain is so uncomfortable I can't stand it another second, I think of the beating I'm going to give the other riders, and suddenly I'm fine."

Opposite: Dealing with some pre-race tension, Bob Hannah and mechanic Brain Lunniss wait for the start of the Seattle Washington Kingdome Supercross in 1983. *TMP*

Above: Always the joker, Hannah laughs it up with the author's wife, Darlene. Hannah was one of the most popular riders ever, simply because he loved to play to the crowd. *TMP*

Due to other commitments I did not attend the next six events. However, Hannah called from time to time and let me know his progress. He was back to the Hannah of old by the time he reached St. Louis, winning both motos and the overall. At Mt. Morris on May 29th, Hannah again won both motos and the overall, and had the points lead well in hand. He showed no mercy at Binghamton, New York, winning both motos and the overall. It looked like the 250cc National Championship would go to Honda.

JUNE 11, 1983,
THOUSAND OAKS, CALIFORNIA

I receive a telephone call late in the evening from Hannah. Things are not going well.

Brian Lunniss, Hannah, and Jeff Hicks had gotten an invitation to ride a practice session and light check before the Supercross at the Tangerine Bowl stadium. Shortly after the session began, Hannah flew toward a jump, overcooked his launch, and had to unload from the bike to keep himself from flying into the grandstands. The result was a badly broken wrist, damaged tailbone, and seriously twisted ankle.

It is midnight when Hannah calls, and he asks if I can pick him up at Los Angeles airport around 3:00 a.m. After staying with us for five days, Honda sends Bob to Japan for special treatment. Using some type of electronic impulse device twenty-four hours a day, doctors try to heal the wrist quickly. The Supercross and Outdoor National titles are at stake.

JUNE 21, 1983,
THOUSAND OAKS, CALIFORNIA

Bob is back in California and tries to resume training. I go with him late at night as he tries a ten-mile run with me riding a road bicycle as a chaser. It is so dark that I can hardly see him running only a few feet in front of me. He never speaks a word for the whole ten miles. He is totally lost in thought about his future.

JULY 3, 1983,
BUCHANAN, MICHIGAN

Bob's wrist is in a half cast and he has super trainer Jeff Spencer tape it as well to see if he can ride the Red Bud Outdoor National. Brian is very depressed. The Honda bosses look worried. Hannah tries, but the pain is too much and he can't get the job done.

JULY 5, 1983,
THOUSAND OAKS, CALIFORNIA

Hannah calls and tells me to cancel plans to go to Pittsburgh or Cincinnati. He thinks the Supercross and Outdoor National titles are lost. It is a very difficult blow to his career; he wanted to win in the worst way. He says, "I'm riding better than ever, and now this. I just can't believe this is happening."

AUGUST 4, 1983,
KETCHUM, IDAHO

My wife and I spend a few days with Hannah, but Team Honda orders him back to Japan for more treatment on his wrist. David Bailey will win both the Supercross title and the 250cc Outdoor National title for Honda. But there are several races to go before the end of the season, and I stay on to track the story.

To go along with the mud and rain, Hannah's mechanic Brian Lunniss flashes the news that, at the 15-minute mark, Bob has an eight-second lead on teammate David Bailey. *TMP*

When asked about the 1983 250cc National at Castle Rock, Colorado, mechanic Brian Lunniss remarked, "It was so hot you couldn't think. Hannah was doing his usual thing—beating the crap out of the competition—when the ignition failed and we ended up with a DNF". *TMP*

Checking the starting line before the first moto at the 1983 AMA 250cc Outdoor National in Castle Rock, Colorado, the new "Hurricane II" gets ready to face the heat and dust of a track so dry that, by the end, fans could hardly tell who was racing. *TMP*

AUGUST 14, 1983, WASHOUGAL, WASHINGTON

Bob has made a recovery and his wrist is doing better.

The track at Washougal is picturesque and the weather is simply prefect, with bright skies and warm temperatures. Hannah will try and salvage his Outdoor National Championship, although his chances of doing so are very slim.

After running one of his competitors off the road in a rental car on the way to the track, Hannah wins moto one, with Rick Johnson second, and Scott Burnworth third.

In moto two, while leading with a lap and a half to go, the Honda breaks a gearbox and puts Hannah on the side of the track. Johnson takes the win and the overall; Hannah finishes eighth overall.

Bob returns to the pit after the second moto. His hands are blistered, and the swelling in his wrist has flared up and he can barely move his hand. The title chances are now gone, and I detect some signs of depression. The season has been very difficult, and Bob wanted to win the championship for Honda and prove to Yamaha they had made a mistake by letting him go.

AUGUST 20, 1983, CASTLE ROCK, COLORADO

I meet up with Bob and Brian as they work on the bike in the parking lot of the Sheraton Inn, Lakewood.

Both Brian and Bob are in the middle of a hassle with the Japanese engineer in charge of the transmission used on the race bike. Still mad from the failure in Washougal, Hannah says, "This gearbox is a piece of crap." The engineer, not a native English speaker, says, "No piece of crap, Bob." Hannah tosses a wrench at the transmission and says, "Piece of crap." The engineer puts his head down and walks off.

The track at Castle Rock is at high altitude, and this affects the performance of the Honda. Track conditions are not suited to Bob's style; no ruts, only a hard-packed, super-fast surface. Temperature on race day is near ninety degrees Fahrenheit before noon, and the dry track produces dust. Bob's wrist and hand are very sore. During practice, a lean condition develops in the engine and, when Bob attempts to clear a giant dropoff, the engine dies. When the bike hits the ground, Bob over-revs the engine and flies over the bars and lands hard. He continues, but is in a lot of pain.

David Bailey wins both motos, and wins the 250cc Outdoor National Championship. There is one race to go in the series; both Bob and Brian are very disappointed.

AUGUST 28, 1983,
MILLVILLE, MINNESOTA

Despite his pain and the overwhelming feeling of depression about losing the 250cc title, Bob rebounds at Millville and wins moto one. He is second to Bailey in moto two, and Bailey wins the overall. It's all too late, and everything is on hold until 1984.

OCTOBER 4, 1983,
THOUSAND OAKS, CALIFORNIA

I receive a telephone call from Brian Lunniss on the evening of October 4 informing me that, while riding in the desert with some friends, Bob had crashed with serious consequences. The bike landed on Bob, breaking his pelvis, dislocating his hip, and damaging his kidney, bladder, and liver. He is in serious, but stable, condition at a hospital in Lancaster, California. The following morning, my wife and I drive to Lancaster.

Arriving at the hospital, we are met by Brian, who then escorts us to Bob's room. Hannah is lying semiconscious, with tubes connecting him to various machines. Brian leaves to make several phone calls, and Darlene and I retreat to a corner of the room and sit down. Several minutes later, two young men come into the room carrying motorcycle helmets and wearing riding gear. They look at Bob, then at us, and inquire if Bob can sign their helmets because they are big fans. We don't get a chance to respond, as Brian returns, goes ballistic, and escorts the two young men out.

NOVEMBER 17, 1983,
THOUSAND OAKS, CALIFORNIA

Bob stays with us while getting treatment. His condition is better, but he is far from recovered. He has difficulty walking, he has nerve damage that is creating problems; the doctors are concerned, telling Hannah there is a chance he can have permanent damage to his internal organs. Hannah alternates between depression and determination.

JANUARY 13, 1984,
EL TORO, CALIFORNIA

It's a new year, and training is going very slowly. Bob's hip and pelvis are very sore, and after every practice session the pain becomes severe. Bob alternates between riding in the desert and at the private track leased by Honda. He is underweight, weak, and not feeling good overall.

He has missed the first Golden State series race, but plans to run one moto at Saddleback Park on January 14th.

JANUARY 28, 1984,
ANAHEIM, CALIFORNIA

There is a record crowd of over 70,000 fans in Anaheim Stadium to watch the Supercross season get under way. Unlike years past, on this evening the fans become unruly; there are fights in the grandstands. Hannah gets the biggest ovation, as the fans go nuts when he is introduced.

Before the race, Bob admits he is not sure of himself. He says he is worried about his conditioning. It is the first time I have ever heard him sound so concerned. I notice a pronounced change in Hannah's personality. He is no longer the wild and fearless kid he was from 1977 to 1979. He is now a man and seems more serious; the carefree smile is less frequent. Johnny "The O' Show" O'Mara wins the main and Hannah finishes tenth.

Although known around the world as a champion on 250cc-class bikes, Bob Hannah earned his bones riding a 125cc, winning a championship in 1976 and returning from time to time to the class as shown in this 1979 shot of him riding at the USGP. *Werner Straub; Terry Good*

Bitter rival to most of his competition through the years, Bob was a mentor to his young Honda teammates, David Bailey and Johnny O'Mara. Here the Hurricane and Bailey wait to get into the starting gate at Castle Rock in Colorado. *TMP*

FEBRUARY 2, 1984,
LANCASTER, CALIFORNIA

Hannah crashes while practicing in the desert and totally destroys a factory works bike. Brian is calling him "Hamburger Hannah" because of the large amount of skin ripped from his hand, shoulder, and forearm. Despite the crash, Hannah goes on to ride the Golden State series and does well.

For much of 1984, Hannah was on the road and not in California. His riding improved and, when injury free, he rode much more strongly than he ever had before. He admitted that the Honda was a great bike, and he felt he could still win championships.

However, he crashed with Keith Bowen and injured his bad wrist. Also, while he was leading at Daytona, the fans pushed a wire fence out into the racing line and Bob caught it, ripping a gaping tear in his forearm.

AUGUST, 1984,
WASHOUGAL, WASHINGTON

After many months, I return to taking notes and photos of the 1984 season. Hannah is much improved since I last saw him race. Hannah is very upbeat and has a "Hurricane II" logo on his riding pants, indicating that he is determined to win. However, the relationship between Honda management and the Hurricane is strained. Pressure from one of the team managers regarding the renewal of Bob's contract is causing concerns.

Above: These shots offers an idea as to how Hannah (25) and his Honda worked together. The action is at the 1985 AMA Outdoor National in Washougal, Washington. Below is a pass by Hannah of teammate Johnny O'Mara (3). *TMP*

Opposite: Bob Hannah (left) and longtime buddy and Honda privateer rider Jo-Jo Keller (right) talk things over at the 1985 Supercross in San Diego, California. *TMP*

SMITH
55
SCOTT
HONDA
KELLER
55
HONDA
HONDA

Rick Johnson breaks a finger in moto one, and Jeff Ward smokes everyone, winning overall.

Something strikes Bob after the race is over: The fans mob Hannah's race hauler as if he has won the race. He signs autographs, jokes around, and plays with the younger kids. He gives away all of his riding gear and when a young crippled boy is brought over to the hauler, Hannah drops everything and spends time with the kid, giving him a helmet and a riding shirt.

JANUARY 26, 1985,
SAN DIEGO, CALIFORNIA

It's a new season, and the Hurricane has grown some facial hair for San Diego.

This race ends up being the worst of Bob Hannah's career. Suddenly, the effects of all the crashes and broken bones have surfaced, his training program has slowed, and Brian Lunniss confides in me that Hannah is having serious problems with his ankles and knees. The other problem facing Brian and Bob is the fact that the bike is not set up because practice has been limited. The result of this accumulation of problems? The Hurricane does not qualify for the main event and, even worse, he does not win the last-chance qualifier. Both Brian and Bob are depressed. This night proves to be one of those critical points in his career.

FEBRUARY 2, 1985,
ANAHEIM, CALIFORNIA

Brian has broken his foot in a mishap at Hondaland and is having trouble working on the bike. Bob is feeling much better and is riding very strong. But, in a quiet moment, Bob tells me he is thinking of retiring.

MARCH 16, 1985,
HUNGRY VALLEY, CALIFORNIA

Bob crashes while practicing and breaks the navicular bone in his hand. He leaves the next day for Idaho to see the famed orthopedic surgeon Dr. Warren Sorenson. The bottom line is that if he does not race Hangtown on March 30th, he can lose the Outdoor National Championship for the second year in a row. A little-known fact is in play. During the '85 season, when Bob was well, he rode stronger than he had ever ridden. He told me he loved the Honda and could have won a lot of races if not for the constant injuries.

MARCH 31, 1985,
RANCHO CORDOVA, CALIFORNIA

Bob tries to ride with his broken hand in order to gather points. Honda's world-class trainer Jeff Spencer tapes his hand and wrist. Spencer remarks to Brian Lunniss that Hannah is a lot like Lance Armstrong when it comes to being determined, but Lance is not as mean as Hannah. All the effort is in vain; Bob cannot hang onto the bars because the track is so rough. He leaves Hangtown without any points.

MAY 11, 1985,
LOS ANGELES, CALIFORNIA

Bob has made up his mind that, if possible, he will not ride any more Supercross races, concentrating his efforts on the 250cc Outdoor National events.

But, Honda may have a different opinion on the races he should ride. Bob hates the Coliseum track. He tells Brian he does not want to jump a quad jump (actually two doubles back to back) and he nearly crashes over a set of doubles. Bob is very upset at his performance in the first moto, and uses a slightly sprained wrist as an excuse for not riding the second moto.

Retirement is on his mind, and he makes an off-the-cuff remark that he doesn't want to fly the jumps with Bailey, Johnson, and the other young riders.

MAY 19, 1985,
HENDERSON, NEVADA

Hannah picks up a second and fifth at the Outdoor National in Nevada. Bob came from fortieth to fifth in the second moto, and the fans went crazy. After the race, he tells me he felt more comfortable and he is riding way stronger and the Honda is working better than it has in a while.

JUNE 2, 1985,
THOUSAND OAKS, CALIFORNIA

After finishing second in Atlanta and fourth at Mt. Morris, Hannah calls my house to tell me in strictest confidence that he has no chance to win the 250cc title. He will finish the season and think about retiring. He says he is burned out.

During his years with Honda and mechanic Brian Lunniss, Hurricane Hannah rode as well as he ever had in his career. Hannah said he loved the bike and felt he could have won a lot of races. This sequence of photos offers up some action at the 1985 250cc Outdoor Nationals at Hangtown near Sacramento, California. *TMP*

DUNLOP

Thank God for Bell Helmets! At any given moment, motocross racing can reach up and bite you hard. In 1987, Hannah crashed his Suzuki and the bike landed on his head, crushing his helmet and resulting in a concussion. *TMP*

As the 1986 season began, I didn't attend any races. Bob had signed with Suzuki, and rode some Supercross events in Italy and France. When Danny "Magoo" Chandler crashed at the Paris Supercross and was paralyzed, it was the realization of every rider's biggest fear.

Brian Lunniss stayed with Honda, and Rick Johnson became his rider—and Bob Hannah became the enemy.

FEBRUARY 11, 1986,
THOUSAND OAKS, CALIFORNIA

I receive a telephone call from Jeff Hicks informing me that Hannah has crashed while testing the new Suzuki. The cause of the crash was the transmission popping out of gear over a double jump. The result of the crash is a broken collarbone (two places), a damaged thumb, and a bruised kidney. Bob stays with us during part of his rehab; he seems depressed, but never really says much.

Opposite: When Hannah went to Suzuki in 1986 he lost Brian Lunniss as a mechanic. Bitter rival Rick Johnson (shown) took over as Honda's rider and Brian Lunniss came along as his mechanic. Johnson and Hannah would never really see things eye to eye; Hannah was the old man and Rick was the new gun. *TMP*

APRIL 6, 1986,
RANCHO CORDOVA, CALIFORNIA

The original plan with Suzuki is to have Hannah ride a testing and development program. They allow him to choose which races he wants to run. He decides to run more races than expected. However, at Hangtown the bike is not right and Hannah is still recovering from a long list of physical problems. The fans have no idea how tough it is for him to ride well.

JULY 20, 1986,
NEW BERLIN, NEW YORK

I don't get to witness Bob's win at Unadilla. Nor do I hear the fans go crazy with joy. But, I do get one story about the race, told to me secondhand. It seems that, during one of the motos, the wife of World Champion Jacky Vimond held up a sign for her husband reading "Hannah Exhausted." Several minutes later, Bob smoked Jacky like he was tied to a tree.

From this point in 1986 until Hannah retired at Unadilla in 1989, I did not attend another motocross event. After his retirement, I was witness to his attempts at open-wheel racing, Formula One boat racing, and his invitation to race at the 1990 Toyota Pro/Celebrity Grand Prix in Long Beach. I also sat helpless during several "mayday" calls when Hannah went airplane racing at Reno, but those are all stories for another chapter.

Here is a very rare sight—Bob Hannah (right) and Johnny "The O'Show" O'Mara on Suzuki motocross bikes. Hannah and O'Mara were teammates at Honda and then, when Bob moved to Suzuki in 1986, the O'Show followed. *TMP*

A mud-covered Hurricane offers a few words to Larry Maiers after a hard-run moto during the 1987 Motocross des Nations. *Larry Maiers*

Don't ride on private property! A friend of Bob's, Big Mike the Cop, played a little gag on Team Honda when invited to watch a practice session. *TMP*

6

THE GOOD TIMES

Although Hannah ran in Europe several times during his career, he never really cared for the place. He missed his home in Idaho and could not get used to the food. In 1978 he was part of the U.S. team at Gaildorf Germany during the running of the Motocross des Nations. *Moto Verte; Terry Good*

From the year 1976 until the mid-1980s, motocross racing in the United States went from a counterculture European import to a full-fledged red, white, and blue phenomenon. The groundswell of enthusiasm had been planted by pioneers like John Penton, Gary Bailey, Brad Lackey, Mark Blackwell, Gary Jones, Jimmy Weinert, Gary Semics, and Jim Pomeroy. Wild, fearless, and free, motocross riders attracted the spirit of youth. As always, motorcycles and young vibrant fans were an explosion waiting to happen.

During this time, one free spirit flew higher than the rest. He became a hero, a legend, and a target at which all would aim. Brash, intemperate, and outrageously talented, he took American motocross to the next level. He rode like a demon, lightning bolts on his helmet, in a style never duplicated. Bob "Hurricane" Hannah reached his pinnacle during this period of motocross hysteria, and fans by the thousands came to witness him cast a spell over the sport.There must have been millions of words written about the career of Bob

Hannah, alongside an equal number of photos. So what is left to say?

Well, the words and photos of journalists like Jody Weisel, Tom Webb, Jim Gianatsis, Dennis Cox, Mark Kariya, Dick Miller, Fran Kuhn, and Rick Seaman were only their points of view. And articles in magazines like *Dirt Bike*, *Moto Cross*, *Motocross Action*, *Super Moto Cross*, *Cycle*, and *Cycle World* offered race coverage and generalization of an overall view. There were a wide variety of opinions. The *Los Angeles Times* reluctantly covered motorcycle racing from two diametrically opposed views. The late (and dyspeptic and moody) Jim Murray called them "murdercycles," but the late (and venerable) Shav Glick wrote glowingly of motocross and the Hurricane.

Some of those who wrote the words thought of Hannah as a superstar, a master of his trade. Many journalists thought of Hannah as rude, arrogant, self-centered, and possessing an attitude filled with ego. But what was the truth? What really happened and who is the real Bob Hannah? The truth is that Hannah never cared to impress the media, and his style has always been one of straight talk, in which he always speaks his mind and never gives an inch when he feels strongly about something.

So the challenge, in telling the story of Bob Hannah's prime, is to separate fact from fiction, truth from exaggeration, and accuracy from bias.

Early in this story, Hannah talked about his childhood, his early days learning to ride, and his love for both his dad, Wild Bill, and his uncle, Mel. From that point onward, the story of Bob Hannah was been told through the memories of some of his closest friends. My own records, compiled between 1983 and 1986, are reasonably close to the truth, but the events are seen through my eyes only. But the pinnacle years were missing one important factor: memories from the man who lived them. Those years were filled with what Hannah has always called "critical points," and it seemed important to get the facts firsthand.

When I suggested that Hannah offer his own words on these pinnacle years, he wasn't sure he could do the job. He admitted, "I can't remember a lot of stuff that happened; there have been so many races and so many places. Parts of it seem like a lifetime ago, and some of it stands out like it was yesterday."

I agreed, but countered by asking for only a taste of the big years, the championships, and the fans. Something, too, about the tough times, the crashes, the move from Yamaha to Honda, and then to Suzuki. About getting old and realizing that his time had reached its climax. The readers have a right to know his side of the story.

That idea is all well and good, but there was one complication to getting Hannah to comply: Hannah is a "now" person. What matters is today.

Living in the moment has always been his style, and I can illustrate the point with a story.

A few years back, at the Air Races in Reno, Nevada, Hannah was flying a highly modified P-51 Mustang in the annual National Air Race event. During his heat race, while flying flat out a hundred feet off the ground, a part tore off the plane sending it into what could have been a death spin. The g-load from the sudden gyration was beyond comprehension, and losing concentration for only a microsecond would mean instant death. However, somehow Hannah fought for and regained control, saving the plane and his life. The next day, he went back into the air—same plane, same course; no fear, no remorse. It was a new day and he had forgotten about history.

In the late 1980s, Hannah wanted to try his skill at open-wheel car racing. He graduated from the Jim Russell Driving School and ran several races, winning one event at Riverside Raceway. However, Hannah was not as lucky as his ex-rival Jeff Ward, who managed to run in the Indy 500. *TMP*

AND NOW, THE REST OF THE STORY
BOB HANNAH

I would definitely say that 1977 was a crazy year for me. To begin with, I won the Florida Winter-AMA series and the AMA Supercross series—on a bone-stock, production 250cc Yamaha. I was also a serious contender in all three classes in the AMA Nationals—125cc, 250cc, and Open—but then Yamaha switched me over to their unreliable works bikes. Constant breakdowns and trying to develop a bike on the racetrack destroyed any shot I had at a national championship. This included the Trans-AMA series, where after two DNFs I lost the championship to Roger DeCoster by just twenty-one points.

When it was all said and done, I became the first rider to win National races in all three classes in just one season. I certainly give a lot of that credit to my mechanic, Keith McCarty. Most guys have one, maybe two, classes of bikes to oversee for a rider. We were campaigning in three different classes simultaneously. And all the while, Yamaha had us testing the works bike, which was a complete disaster for us both.

By 1978, I could ride with anybody. And the more I won, the more other riders started gunning for me. When I won five straight, talk was that I wouldn't win six. Then when I won eight, they'd say, "He'll never go to ten." It was like pouring gasoline on a fire. All it did was motivate me to train harder, ride more, and give them each an ass whipping. I also knew that with Keith as my mechanic I never had to worry about the bike—he wanted to win as bad as I did, even when it came to beating my own teammates.

For the '78 outdoor season, the AMA announced that each rider could only enter one class in the National Championship series, so Yamaha made the decision for me to focus on the 250 class.

By the end of the '78 season, I'd won four titles: the Florida Winter-AMA series, the Supercross series, the 250cc Outdoor National championship, and the Trans-AMA series (where I became the first American to claim the title over a European). And I won this crazy

This and next two pages: All of the championships won by Bob Hannah took place during his years with Team Yamaha. In 1977, Hannah won the 250cc Supercross title. In 1978, he won the 250cc Supercross and Outdoor National titles. *Steve Reyes*

YAMAHA
4

race called the Motorcycle Olympiad, where they had five different styles of motorcycle racing—with one overall winner—held over two days at Saddleback Park. It was a fun event the AMA put on for a few years. To top off our year, Keith and I were invited to be part of the U.S. team at the Motocross and Trophie des Nations, over in Germany and Belgium.

When the 1979 season started, we picked up right where we left off—winning. I was riding better than I had ever ridden in my life, and Keith and I, along with the Yamaha engineers, had the bike dialed in perfectly.

Guys like Weinert, Tripes, Barnett, and Howerton all wanted a piece of me. They wanted to win as bad as I did. But for other guys, I started to get in their heads. When I'd come up behind them during a race, they wouldn't put up much of a fight, they'd just move over. But if I came up behind you and you didn't move over, then you were just a roadblock and I might have helped you move out of the way.

When Hannah first turned professional, he had never really raced in the mud, as had his competition from the east. After struggling a few times, he made up his mind to train in the mud until he got good. The result, according to Hannah, made him an excellent mud racer. *TMP*

Left: If any photo of Bob Hannah could illustrate his riding style, this shot, taken at Mid-Ohio during the Trans-USA 250cc class in 1981, would be the one. Hannah claimed he didn't have the style of other riders, but his fans will tell you that he rode with desire and that's what they liked. *Werner Straub; Terry Good*

I wasn't the type of rider to start crap with another rider. But if you hit me and I thought it was uncalled for, I'd hit you back even harder. I've been quoted many times throughout my career as saying, "You start it; I'll finish it."

As long as we're talking about starting crap, I had no personal issue with the press. But I didn't chase after them, and some of the journalists didn't like the idea that I wasn't eager to talk to them. Those were some pretty wild days back then, and I've had some crazy things happen to me with guys that abused their positions because of the power they thought they had with their pens. I've been blackmailed before, threatened, you name it. I've seen guys retire prematurely because they couldn't take the BS from certain writers. I had a

Below: In the very small circle of people whom Hannah called "friend" during his racing career, Marty Tripes is one of those listed near the top. Marty was a fantastic rider, with tremendous natural talent. He rode for Team Honda when Hannah rode for Team Yamaha. Tripes thrilled fans in the early days of the Supercross series by putting a whipping on the European riders. *Motocross Action Magazine*

Throughout his career, Bob Hannah was always a crowd favorite. He was outspoken, aggressive, and would never give up and that appealed to the masses who cheered for him. At the 1985 Supercross in San Diego, California, the Hannah fans were out in force. *TMP*

journalist tell me one day that, if I didn't do what he said, he wouldn't write about me in his magazine any more. I told him I didn't give a crap, because as long as I was winning he'd have to write about me or write about second place. So call it what you want. I believe I cooperated with the press. But winning was what I lived for, not magazine stories.

I'll tell you what I did always really enjoy and appreciate: I loved my fans. It was great to have the crowds and the fans behind me. I was always the last guy at the track at any given race, and I made sure every fan got an autograph. More often than not, I gave away my race trophy to some kid in crowd, and I always gave away all my race gear.

By the end of the '79 race season, I picked up my third Supercross Championship in a row, and my second 250 Outdoor National Championship in a row. I was on top of my game. And as the season came to an end, I knew I had a shot at a lot more titles before the end of my career.

One week after I won the '79 250 National Championship, I broke my right leg in 12 places, from the ankle to the knee, water-skiing on the Colorado River. I was out playing around with Marty Tripes and some friends, and the next thing you know, my whole career could've potentially gone out the window. It was just a dumb move on my part. Lesson learned: don't go water-skiing on the Colorado River. If you do, make sure you're driving the boat!

To the Hurricane, winning was the reason he raced. Running second was the same as losing, so if winning meant running through mud without goggles, then that's the way it would be. Here's how it was at Red Bud in 1978. *Werner Straub; Terry Good*

I was out for almost an entire year. During the healing process, my leg became infected and there was talk about possibly having to amputate it, but my doctor was able to hollow out the bone and leave just enough behind in order to save the leg.

My pain threshold is high when I'm in perfect shape, but after my accident, and after having a full year off, I was far from being in perfect shape. As soon as I could, I started weight training. I worked on a speed bag, then a heavy bag, just like a fighter. When I finally got clearance from the doctors, I started running. I gained a little every day and eventually I worked my way back up to ten miles a day.

The first time I got back on the bike, it seemed a little strange. But after eight or ten weeks of riding six days a week, things really started to come around. Being so far out of shape, it was hard to gauge my progress. Not having raced for so long, you lose your edge, and the biggest problem becomes timing. When you lose your timing, it forces you to think about what you have to do, instead of everything being automatic. But after about five months of riding and training, everything started to come back around for me.

All along, I had Keith right there to help get me back on my feet and back on top. What never changed throughout the entire year I was off was my desire to win, my drive and determination. I *still* hated running for second or third. And so did Keith.

Unfortunately, it seemed like the year I'd taken off for my broken leg in 1980, Yamaha had also taken off in the development of the bike. My welcome back gift was a 30-pounds-too-heavy tub-of-crap bike that wasn't worthy of competition. There was no way I stood a chance with that thing. I don't know what the engineers were thinking. That year, Honda and Suzuki got serious about

After many operations and nearly a year of rehab, Bob Hannah recovered from a shattered leg that came close to ending his riding career. He returned to racing at the 1980 Trans-USA race at Mid-Ohio. *Werner Straub; Terry Good*

weight and went to the limit in cutting pounds. I tried to tell upper management that their bikes were too heavy, but they just told Broc Glover and me that we were out of shape and didn't know what we were talking about.

My results spoke for themselves in '81—I could hardly put anything together. How do you tell guys who sit at desks all day that their bikes suck? I tried, but they didn't listen.

In 1982, Yamaha paid me an extra hundred grand to ride their 125. The reason was simple: they had an overstock of bikes and they knew if I rode one—win, lose, or draw—they would sell out the entire warehouse. They also promised me that if I rode it, they'd back me one hundred percent with anything I needed for the bike, with full support from Japan. Unfortunately, they didn't keep their word, and once again the results spoke for themselves. The bike was constantly breaking down during competition. It was a piece of junk.

By the end of '82, I'd made up my mind and left Yamaha for Honda. Over the years, they had treated me fair, and Keith McCarty had given me his best, but my commitment was always to winning, and I felt that Yamaha no longer shared that commitment. It was tough losing Keith, but I understood that he had a family he needed to look out for first and foremost. Yamaha was lucky to keep him.

I'd won seven national titles with Yamaha, had a bunch of great times, and made a lifelong friend in Keith before I moved on. Not bad.

In 1983, I was in better shape than I was at any other time in my career. And fortunately for me, Honda had not only put tremendous effort into their bikes, they'd also provided me with an extremely dedicated mechanic, Brian Lunniss, whom I'd known since my early days as a test rider for Suzuki.

continued on page 142

BRIAN LUNNISS

DURING HIS YEARS WITH HONDA, Bob Hannah openly admitted that it was the best of times and the worst of times. When he was on his game, he considered himself unbeatable. He confided that he was in better condition and rode better during his Honda years than at any other time in his career. The bikes were awesome and he once remarked, "Anyone who couldn't win on a Honda should just go home."

The move from Yamaha to Honda posed one major problem for Hannah. He had always depended on Keith McCarty to prepare his bikes. Keith was one of the best in the business, and without a great mechanic a rider can't perform at his peak. The choice Bob made was Brian Lunniss, and the pairing could not have been a better partnership. Brian was meticulous in his labor, and possessed the same fire and determination for winning as Hannah.

BRIAN LUNNISS

My introduction to Bob Hannah occurred while I was working for Suzuki as a racing mechanic back in 1974–'75. At the time, we were testing production RM bikes at Saddleback, one of the local tracks. We had two factory riders, Billy Grossi and Tony DiStefano, working with several privateer riders in the events. Bob was there racing his own Husky, and I couldn't believe how fast he was riding. He impressed everyone, including the Suzuki team manager. Bob ended up testing with us, and Suzuki then allowed him to ride local events as a support rider.

When Donnie Hansen got hurt in 1982, it left a space open on the Honda Team and, in 1983, Bob was hired. He picked me as his mechanic, because I had stayed in contact with him and we had remained friends. Honda looked to Bob as an experienced champion with much to offer the team. Bob added an extra dimension to David Bailey and Johnny O'Mara. Both Roger DeCoster and Dave Arnold were excited, but there were rumors that Bob was washed up, over the hill and that is the reason

In 1983 Hannah had moved to Honda and had a new mechanic named Brian Lunniss. The two were a great team and won the famed Daytona Supercross in 1983 and 1985. Shown here, Brian, sitting on Hannah's race bike, enjoys a moment in the winner's circle as Bob looks on. *Brian Lunniss Collection*

he and Yamaha had parted company. Not true; Bob had fully recovered from his leg and he was ready to prove that he was better than ever. The truth is that Bob was so driven to prove he was not washed up that when we started the season at the Florida series, Bob simply abused the competition. The same thing happened in California. From the time we began testing, I could see that the Honda fit Bob's style perfectly. He was riding at his peak and then some. Everyone who knows Hannah can tell you, when he is in shape and riding at his best, it spells trouble for anyone in his way.

By midseason, 1983, we were leading the Supercross and the Outdoor National championships. Bob was using the field for target practice. He was going to give Honda both titles. Then, in a practice session just before the Orlando Supercross, he crashed and broke his wrist. Both championships went down the toilet.

Honda was winning the National Outdoor Championship with David Bailey and Dave Arnold and Roger came up and asked if Bob could help David in his quest of the title. At the next National, Bob went out in the first moto and won going away. When the second moto started, Bob charged to the front and Dave and Roger are having a shit fit. At the end of the race, Bob let David by. Bailey passed him and won the moto and the title. Everybody knew Bob had the race covered, but when asked about it, he just smiled.

In the years Bob rode for Honda, it was the heyday of the works bike, so I would build a bike exactly the way Bob wanted it to be. It fit his style to perfection. His preferences were totally different than those of Bailey or O'Mara. When we started working together, Bob was so driven and focused that I would have five bikes ready at all times, so he could go riding whenever and wherever he wanted. He was the only rider I ever worked with who was so totally self-motivated.

He had his own schedule, and I had to be ready. He would say, "Tomorrow we're leaving to go ride at 7:00 a.m.," or "We're going to the desert and do an all-day workout." Some days we would do two or three motos at the Honda test track, then he would go home and begin a late-day workout. He was obsessed with winning. Nobody in the sport worked harder.

I don't think Bob ever believed in how good he really was. He would say, "If I had as much talent as O'Mara or Bailey, I'd kill the competition." He always believed that his style of riding was not as smooth and perfect as other riders'.

The truth of how good Bob would have been and how many championships he could have won during his Honda years will never be known, because he was cursed by injuries. He broke his wrist and then he started having trouble with his ankles. He would use three rolls of tape just to tape his ankles before he rode. Every time Bob would get to one hundred percent and start winning, there would be another crash. Then there was his crash in the desert that broke his pelvis. I can tell you as a witness, that incident was far more serious than anyone will ever know.

At the end of the 1985 season, certain people in Honda upper management lost interest in Bob and rumors again surfaced about Hannah being washed up as a championship contender. DeCoster and Arnold knew that Bob was not washed up. Bob has told me that he loved Honda and he would have never left. But he felt that he was being jerked around by management and, before I knew what happened, Hannah and Honda parted company.

Bob went to Suzuki and I teamed with Rick Johnson. When I look back at Honda and Hannah, I remember certain things he would say. Asked about why he rode so hard, he would say, "You have to take the wins whenever you can get them, because you never know what might happen." He would follow up by saying, "I want to beat guys so bad that, when I walk through the pit area, they look down at their feet." Bob wanted to win every time; he hated losing. He hated getting hurt, because he knew that injuries could end his career. Although he never expressed himself openly, I always felt that what happened to Donnie Hansen, David Bailey, and Danny Chandler had a profound effect on him.

In 2008, I ran into Jeff Spencer, a professional trainer who had once worked with Bob in getting over his injuries. When recalling Hannah, Spencer said, "Hannah and Lance Armstrong had much the same kind of personality when they raced, except Lance was a little more refined than the Hurricane."

In the end, Bob Hannah was the greatest racer I ever dealt with because he raced to win every time. He never left anything on the table.

Brian Lunniss and Bob Hannah tried to create a game plan for the 1985 Supercross at the Los Angeles Coliseum. Lunniss once remarked, "The Los Angeles Coliseum was never very kind to us." *TMP*

Hannah
HRC
25
DUNLOP
SMITH
FLAK JAK 2
WIGLOW
467
RICHARDSON

continued from page 137

At the start of the '83 season, everything came together. I was killing them. Guys like Howerton and others who were whipping my butt in '82 were nowhere to be found in '83. I was leading both the Supercross and the 250 Nationals when I broke my wrist doing a totally uncalled for jump during a test session in Orlando. It cost me both championships.

It was just my luck—or lack of it—that in 1983 I was in the best shape of my life, but I didn't win a championship. I was riding better, training harder, and the Honda bikes were perfect. But a series of injuries continued to plague me. If I'd remained injury free, there is no doubt in my mind that I would have done better on the Honda than I had on the Yamaha. I would always say, if you couldn't win on a Honda, it was time to go home.

At the end of the '83 season, I broke my pelvis and suffered some internal injuries as a result of the accident. At the time, I kept the extent of my injuries hidden because I was still looking to re-sign with Honda. But once I was able to negotiate a contract for another two years, you can bet the pressure was on for me to perform.

I blew it. I ended up coming back too soon in '84. My body hadn't had a chance to heal properly from the pelvis injury, and that hurt my ability to go all out. Then bad luck just continued to chase me down during my remaining two years with Honda. It was one injury after another. I had a great bike, a great mechanic, I spent all my time training, but I couldn't catch a break. I certainly produced a number of wins, but there would be no championships for me on a Honda.

As the '85 season ended, I had a major decision to make. I would've loved to have stayed with Honda a few more years, but I had a problem with some folks in upper management. So, ultimately, I made the decision to go ahead and let my contract expire without any fanfare. Plus, thoughts of retirement had started to creep into my head, so now seemed as good a time as any to call it a day.

But right about the time I was trying to make an exit, I got a call from an old boss of mine from my early days at Suzuki in '75. It was Shiginoya, asking if I'd come over and help them develop their bikes and do some PR work for the company. So, in '86, I signed a two-year deal—which ultimately lasted until around '93.

By late 1981, Hannah had recovered from his leg injury and was back with Team Yamaha. I approached Hannah about doing a book at the time; the answer was "Not ready yet." *Darlene Madigan*

When Hannah was on his game, he could be a blur to the competition. During his years at Honda, he and his mechanic Brian Lunniss believed he could have won several more championships had it not been for injuries. *TMP*

BELL
43

For the first couple of years, I rode a few Nationals of my choosing, strictly for bike testing. Suzuki also asked me to participate in a few events at Unadilla, known to be my favorite track. One was the '86 Unadilla 250 USGP, where lady luck finally turned in my direction and I got my first win ever on the rugged track. I rode a Boyesen Link modified RM250 that day. Then, in '87, I rode an RM125 for the US Team at the Motocross des Nations at Unadilla, and pulled off a win in the worst conditions imaginable—mud, rain, wind, you name it. Probably the sweetest win of my career. Our whole team won that day. So to top it off, we got a chance to meet one of my heroes, President Ronald Reagan.

The President of the United States meets the Hurricane. Ronald Reagan shakes hands with Bob Hannah, member of the winning 1987 U.S. Motocross des Nations team. *White House PR*

Opposite: The original plan when Bob finally went back to Suzuki was to have him test and develop bikes. However, Hannah couldn't stand being on the sidelines, and soon he was back in the fight. *TMP*

In 1988, I headed overseas to France and competed in a couple of events. I won the Paris Supercross and placed second in the French Grand Prix. By this time, I was spending a lot of time in Japan with Suzuki engineers and less time on the racetrack. Suzuki also had me working with all their young riders, developing their new factory recruits.

By 1989, I knew I needed to make an official retirement announcement. My fans had always meant the world to me, and I felt like they deserved some kind of official send-off. There was no better place to do this than Unadilla! The best Bob Hannah fans on the planet were always at Unadilla, so there was no question that I wanted to put an end to my racing days right there, on my favorite track with my favorite fans. And they didn't disappoint.

Even though I was done with racing, I wasn't finished with Suzuki. In the early '90s, I started working with ESPN—via Suzuki—doing color commentary for the AMA National Motocross and Supercross races. I also did some stuff with ESPN's *MotoWorld*, and got a chance to work with my good friend Larry Maiers. You might even be able to dig up a few episodes of Suzuki's *Great Outdoors*.

Somewhere in there, I played around with some open wheel car racing and some Formula One boat racing. But it wasn't until a friend of mine gave me the opportunity to fly a P-51 Mustang that I was forever bitten by the warbird bug. Once I started flying warbirds and discovered I could race them around pylons at speeds close to 500 miles per hour as low as 30 feet off the ground with up to eight other guys all around me, all bets were off. Forget it. I was going flying, and nothing else.

In 1995, I was given an opportunity of a lifetime when a gentleman named Bob Button asked me if I'd like to fly his modified P-51 Mustang *Voodoo Chile*—now just called *Voodoo*—in the Unlimited Class at the Reno Air Races. It was the best six years of adrenaline rushes a guy could ask for. "Mayday King" was my nickname! And the pay wasn't half bad either—a buck a year! I have my final paycheck framed in my office today. Six bucks!

Voodoo still flies around the pylons every year at Reno, but now the owner flies her himself, which is great. We're still great friends, and I'll forever be grateful to him for giving me the ride of my life.

Today, I spend my time working on my two aviation companies, Bob Hannah Aviation and Northwest Backcountry Aircraft. I don't have to travel much anymore, so that leaves a lot of time to spend with my wife, Terri, and our two golden retrievers, Willie and Gracie. I'm doing exactly what I want to do in life: hanging out with my family and friends, flying, hunting, running my own business, riding my Harley with Hicks and Hartnett—what more can a guy ask for? Life is grand for the ol' Hurricane.

Above and opposite page: Shortly before his retirement from active racing as a professional motocross rider, Hannah attended the Jim Russell Driving School at the famed Laguna Seca racetrack near Monterey, California. One of his classmates was Johnny Unser (shown with Bob opposite page, top left), who went on to run the Indy 500 several times. *TMP*

Jim Russell
SCHOLARSHIP TEAM

125/250 cc CHAMPIONSHIP
YAMAHA * COORS
MOTOCROSS
Sunday, April 4, 1982 - 1:00 p.m.
Saddleback Park, Orange, CA.
PARK PASS - THIS IS NOT A TICKET
OBTAIN A GATE PASS AT FRONT GATE IF YOU HAVE TO LEAVE THE PARK
THIS PASS GOOD IN DESIGNATED AREAS
OBEY ALL OFFICIALS
NOT TRANSFERRABLE
STAFF
№ 106
THE YAMAHA GOLD CUP
SUPERCROSS
Presented by The Seattle Times
SEATTLE KINGDOME
SUN. FEBRUARY 14, 1982
1:00PM
FIELD
AMA
CCESS PIT & TRACK ONLY
HANGTOWN
APRIL 8
AMA NATIONAL MOTOCROSS
PIT PASS № 0982
84
CMC NO. 48
Name Rob Hannah
1983
MX
DIRT TRACK
MINI 85cc 9-11 12-16
JR CYCLE 60cc Thru 8 9-11
VETS/ O.T.
A.T.V.
Jr
Int
Pro
Ex
Mstrs
EXPIRES DECEMBER 31, 1983
January 31, 1987 • Anaheim Stad
ISTICS ANA '8
ate 3 or Tunnel 8. Re-entry through any gate.
d for admission. Unrestricted in all areas.
SUZUKI
Southern California Bank
KHJ-TV
172
SIGNATURE
MEMBERSHIP CARD
AMA No.
AMA
AMERICAN MOTORCYCLIST ASSOCIATION
ROBERT HANNAH
2194 EMPIRE RANCH RD
CARSON CITY NV 89701
YEAR MEMBER
EXPIRES LAST DAY OF
P.O. Box 141 • Westerville, Ohio 43081
, 1990
9:00 a.m.
AL ADMISSION
void if detached
2434
GENERAL ADMISSION
ENTER ANY GATE
CART / PPG INDY CAR WORLD SERIES
TOYOTA GRAND PRIX OF LONG BEACH
GENERAL ADMISSION
APRIL 20, 21, 22, 1990
Adult $25
NO REFUNDS FOR LATE ARRIVALS
NO REFUNDS OR EXCHANGES
ATURDAY, APRIL 21, 1990
EVENTS START 8:00 a.m.
GENERAL ADMISSION
void if detached
RIDAY, APRIL 20, 1990
EVENTS START 8:00 a.m.
GENERAL ADMISSION
void if detached
HANGTOWN
MARCH 31
AMA NATIONAL MOTOCROSS
PIT PASS № 1137
85
KICKOFF
1985 • San Diego Jack Murphy Stadium
SD '85
lot only. Restricted to Infield and Pit areas prior to 7:00 p.m. After 7:00 p.m. restricted to Pit area only.
KGB-FM
Castrol
Coca-Cola
AMAHA
Radisson Hotel
000278
SECTION ROW SEAT
7 47 104
JULY 11, 1981
ADMIT ONE THIS DATE ONLY
KMET WELCOMES THE Sprite
SUPERBOWL OF MOTOCROSS
HONDA
Schlitz
L.A. COLISEUM / SATURDAY / JULY 11, 1981
GATES OPEN 6:30 P.M. / RACING 8:00 P.M.
Rain Or Shine
NO REFUND PRICE NO EXCHANGE
$25.00 ADULT RESERVE
SECTION $12.50 CHILD
SPECIAL DISC.
$25.00 NO DISCOUNT
JULY 11, 1981

Above: The responsibilities of racing on the world stage, staying in condition, and overcoming injuries turned the Hurricane from a wild child to a mature man who made his mark as a champion. *TMP*

Opposite: Just a drop of remnants from the bucket of a professional motocross racer's career. *TMP; Bob Hannah*

Hannah gets ready for a little jet training under the watchful eye of Mira Slovak. Ageless, Mira was an airline pilot, an unlimited hydroplane boat racing champion and, oh by the way, he once took over the controls of a Czechoslovakian airliner and flew to freedom from his communist homeland. *TMP*

7

WFO IN THE AFTERLIFE OF MOTOCROSS

Bob Hannah (left) visits with old buddy Larry Maiers on the set of *MotoWorld*, a motocross and motorcycle show hosted by Larry on ESPN. *Larry Maiers*

For several years after his retirement, Hannah seemed to be carefully searching his inner being, attempting to fill the gaps created when he left the sport he had taken to the next level here in the United States. Automobile racing, at the level Bob wanted to enter, required strong personal sponsorship support along with a substantial background in four-wheel racing. Several motorcycle stars had made the transition over the years: Mike "The Bike" Hailwood, Eddie Lawson, Joe Leonard, and Jeff Ward, to mention a few. But for Hannah, the right situation never evolved.

There was some television work with ESPN and with Larry Maiers and his show *MotoWorld*. As he mentioned earlier, Hannah teamed with the Gillman family racing boats. The Gillman family had been deeply involved with motocross prior to their boat racing venture. Bob said that he really enjoyed the action of Formula boat racing.

Hannah continued to develop as an airplane pilot. Flying became a challenge for Bob, and the more he flew, the more he challenged himself. Remember how Bob Hannah used total determination and dedication to become a motocross champion? Flying provided the same demands.

For those who know Bob Hannah, that flying would captivate his drive toward perfection was easy to predict. Soon, mundane flying machines, like his Cessna 210, gave way to a single-seat, two-winged Pitts aerobatic, high performance stunt plane. Hannah began flying aerobatic contests and immediately went to the top of the list in performance.

continued on page 157

THE CALMING EFFECT

SWEET T / TERRI HANNAH

IN NATURE, THE MOST TURBULENT STORM, THE MOST FEROCIOUS OF WINDS, THE DARKEST OF SKIES WILL, AT SOME POINT, BECOME CALM. So it was with a Hurricane named Hannah. In the beginning, his restless spirit created a powerful blast of rebelliousness throughout the world of motocross. And, for more than a decade, the Hurricane showed no mercy to those in his path.

His attitude was to win at all costs and never give an inch to the enemy. And, above all, he never let anyone see a weakness.

But in 1986, the Hurricane came across a burst of warm, gentle pressure. This tranquilizing force appeared in the form of a woman. As opposites attract, he came from the wilds of the Mojave Desert and she came from the Heartland of America. Her name was Terri and, in time, she became his wife. Today, Bob and Terri Hannah live in what many would call a perfect harmony. She is the calming effect on the once unrestrained Hurricane.

TERRI HANNAH

Our first encounter was at the Millville National, in my home state of Minnesota, in 1985. The crowd all knew him as "The Hurricane," but this being my first motocross event, Bob was just another rider. A friend of mine, also a motocross racer, suckered me into getting his race jersey signed by Bob.

I remember it like it was yesterday. It wasn't like I was approaching one of *my* idols as I approached this guy sitting comfortably, low to the ground, holding court with a group of friends between motos. I came up from behind and tapped him on the shoulder. He glanced up as if to say, "Yes?" I could feel the group glaring at me. I choked out, "Mr. Hannah, if I'm not bothering you, could I please ask you to sign this jersey?"

Terri and Bob have a strong relationship, and both enjoy the freedom that comes with flying. The couple spends many weekends in the outback, far from the bright lights of the city, camping and exploring places only a bush pilot can find. *Bob Hannah*

There's nothing like a good, old-fashioned back rub. Bob and Terri Hannah goof off for the camera in front of Bob's hanger on the ranch in Idaho. *TMP*

It felt like he took an extended vacation before he gave me a reply. But then he came back with, "And what if you are?" It felt like I was having an out-of-body experience! Bob's face was stoic and dead serious, and nobody in the group moved. It seemed as if time stood still. I went from 5 foot 6 inches and nineteen years old to about a 2-inch tall baby in a nanosecond! But before I could figure out my escape, Bob cracked a smile, and everyone—including me—was in tears with laughter. He made me laugh that very first day, and he's been making me laugh ever since. Millville '85 wouldn't be my last race, but it would prove to be Bob's last outdoor AMA Outdoor National victory. So, looking back, it makes the day all that more special for both of us.

People often tease me about what it must be like to live with the Hurricane, but I'll let you in on a little secret. The hero Bob Hannah may have been on the racetrack to thousands of fans around the world isn't half the hero he's turned out to be off the racetrack as a man! He's big-hearted, committed, loving, and protective of me and our family. And what's always made our relationship so great over the years is the fact that we're best friends, so we love hanging out with each other. We work together, play together, and spend nearly all our time together.

I also think one of our secrets to being so happy and balanced is that we've always had a few beautiful golden retrievers running around our house. Our lives are literally centered around them. They are the final piece of what makes up our "family." And you'll never find a better doggy-daddy than Bob. Our friends always joke that in their next life they want to come back as one of Bob's dogs!

What I've always admired most about Bob is the fact that he's never forgotten where he's come from: a family with little means in the deserts of California. And for all the championships and all the years he's put into racing, Bob's never seen himself as any kind of hero. Matter of fact, he's always been uncomfortable with the title. To him, the only heroes we have in this country are the men and women in uniform. He would just as well spend a day talking with a World War II vet than anyone else you could imagine. But Bob consider *himself* a hero? No way.

I've seen writers and fellow competitors refer to him as arrogant, but it's never a fan who refers to him that way, because Bob has always been fabulous with his fans—still is to this day. He's always considered himself as being no different than the guy leaning over the fence cheering him on. It's just that one day, back in the '70s, he got a lucky break.

Airplanes have replaced motocross for the Hurricane and he now owns his own aviation company. Hannah is shown here with his wife, Terri, and his backcountry bush plane (Bush Hawk) in 2006. *TMP*

He is as spirited and energetic today as the seventeen-year-old kid who left the desert for the dirt to take on the world. He's as conservative and witty as his beloved Rush Limbaugh. He's always been a teller of the truth—like it or not. "Politically incorrect and damn proud of it," is Bob's motto. He lives his life with honor and integrity. He's incredibly smart and driven to succeed. He'll never slow down and never settle for anything but the best—just like the Hurricane, just like Bob Hannah.

He's always treated me like a princess, even when I don't deserve it. He's my John Wayne, my James Dean, my Crocodile Dundee, my Maverick, my Old Yeller, *my Hurricane, MY SCHWEETIE*! I thank God every day that I have him, and I'll love him till the end of time!

P92-J
TECNAM

Above and following page: The Blue Angels tried to "puke" Hannah when they took him for a thrill ride. Everyone knew who the Hurricane was, and they all wanted to take him up and fill his burp bag. To his credit, Hannah's bag stayed empty. *TMP*

Opposite: Once Hannah learned to fly, he wanted to go as far as he could. That included taking a ride in some World War II Warbirds and getting a lesson from legendary aviation pioneer Mira Slovak. *TMP*

continued from page 152

Soon his craving for more brought him to enter the world of warbirds—restored World War II fighter planes. At their best, in combat, these monsters of the sky were stone cold killers of both the enemy and those behind their controls. Hannah pushed himself to his limits and learned a new game. Flying warbirds put him as far from motocross racing as he ever thought possible. He had now met and called "friend" several ex-NASA astronauts. Hannah drew interest from a man named David Price, owner of the Santa Monica Museum of Flying, who offered Bob the chance to fly a number of his personal birds. During a visit to the Santa Paula Airport in Santa Paula, California, a place famous for housing wild experimental aircraft, Hannah was introduced to, and took a lesson from, aviation pioneer and adventurer Mira Slovak.

Hannah reacted to flying like water to a sponge: he became totally absorbed. After making a motorcycle safety film for the U.S. Navy, Hannah was invited to fly with the Blue Angels. The relationship was a natural. The pilots knew the Hurricane, and they wanted to offer him the best ride they could. So, during that ride (resulting in an hour of g-loads and a couple of gray-outs), Hannah got to handle the F-18's controls.

It was only a matter of time until flying high-performance aircraft became racing high-performance aircraft.

To an outsider like me, the National Air Races held in Reno, Nevada, are stunning to witness and difficult to understand, and they offer sensations not found in any other type of racing. I missed Hannah's first air race in 1995, when he flew a stock P-47. Then Bob made the switch from the Bronze Unlimited class to the Gold Unlimited class, upgrading from the P-47 to a highly modified P-51 Mustang. Owned by a man named Bob Button, owner of a California-based trucking company, the Mustang, named *Voodoo*, was an all-out race plane capable of speeds near 500 miles per hour. I went to several test sessions prior to the Reno air races, and learned early on that those who flew racing airplanes were a breed apart from the normal human species.

Above and opposite page: Life after motocross included Unlimited Class air racing for the Hurricane. Throughout the late 1990s and into 2000, Hannah flew *Voodoo*, a highly modified P-51 fighter plane. Air racing, like motocross, made Hannah fearless, aggressive, and highly motivated to stay alive. *TMP*

If you think motocross racing is tough on the old body, then try flying at 500 miles per hour a couple hundred feet off the ground. Here, pilot Bob Hannah gets ready to fly a test run in his P-51 Mustang, *Voodoo*, at a private airport near Ione, California. *TMP*

In fact, my best example of the world of air racing came when I met with Hannah in the desert town of Mojave, California. The airport at Mojave is home to many experimental aircraft companies, unlimited class racing teams, and Burt Rutan's Scaled Composites Corporation (builders of SpaceShipOne and the GlobalFlyer). At lunch, Hannah was surrounded by a gathering of pilots who had all come to Mojave to practice for the upcoming Reno race. Among them were ex-fighter pilots, an ex-astronaut, and a couple of test pilots. Never in all my life had I ever experienced men who were so intense, calculating, and devoid of fear. (There is *fearlessness* and there is *devoid of fear*; the difference is frightening to the neophyte.) I sat spellbound, staring at men who had faced challenges all but a handful of us mortal men would ever know. Their eyes were clear and as cold as ice. As my mind wandered, the thought came: maybe motocross champion Bob Hannah had entered a place too ominous for even his personality. He seemed oddly out of character.

My experience with air racing lasted only three outings: one practice session and two actual Reno events. At a practice test in Ione, California, Bob took *Voodoo* up only to have an engine failure (fuel pump) followed by a "dead stick" landing. At Reno, Bob experienced a near fatal incident and an engine fire that filled the cockpit with smoke, both resulting in "mayday" emergencies and total terror on my part. After witnessing the two Reno events, I gave up—much to the dismay of Button and Hannah.

Bob continued to race Reno for a few more years before deciding to focus more on his business, Bob Hannah Aviation. Today, Bob "Hurricane" Hannah, Motocross Champion, spends his time selling and

You are looking at the face of a pilot that has just made a "dead stick" landing in a modified P-51 after an engine failure. In 1999 while practicing for the Reno Air Races, Hannah experienced an engine failure on his race plane and had to land without power, not an easy thing to do. *TMP*

brokering sales of aircraft of all types. In addition to his airplane dealership, he has other ventures in his home state of Idaho. Hannah says, "I like fun flying with my wife, Terri. We spend time exploring places you can only get to by flying a bush plane. And I still like hunting and fishing. Once a year, a bunch of my friends get together and we ride Harleys on a road trip. But, mainly I like hanging out with Terri on the ranch." As for his racing career, Hannah says he is happy leaving what he did for the history books, this one included.

Hannah's participation in the Toyota Pro/Celebrity Race in 1990 was not a pretty sight. He raced as a pro, along with Bobby Rahal, Johnny Rutherford, and Chip Hanauer. *TMP*

8

THE LONG BEACH CELEBRITY FIASCO

While rehashing the Hannah story and my personal experience with both his career and the years after, I decided I would tell my favorite Hannah story. I pondered my options and, much to my own astonishment, my final choice has nothing to do with motocross racing.

The time was 1990, one year after Hannah had retired from professional motocross racing, and the location was Long Beach, California. The purpose was Bob's participation in the Toyota Pro/Celebrity Race, run as part of the Toyota Grand Prix of Long Beach weekend.

As a magazine editor, I had attended all of the Long Beach Grand Prix races since its inception. In 1977, Toyota Motor Sales conceived the idea of running a special event in which professional racing stars were pitted against celebrity personalities from TV, movies, and sports in a race using modified versions of Toyota production vehicles. Obviously there would have to be some type of handicap to prevent the professional racers from running away, so the field was set by starting the professional racers thirty seconds behind the celebrities.

Over the years, many famous names have graced the lineup, including John Elway, Clint Eastwood, Gene Hackman, James Brolin, Bruce Jenner, astronaut Pete Conrad, Joe Montana, Parnelli Jones, Al Unser, Dan Gurney, Mary Lou Retton, and Danica Patrick, just to mention a few. I had once mentioned to Toyota Public Relations that Bob Hannah might make a good choice for the event, but nothing was promised. Then in 1990, with or without my influence, Hannah was picked as a member of the "celebrity" racers category. He was bumped up to the "professional" category after qualifying second behind Bobby Rahal. "Maybe I should have sandbagged it," Hannah suggested later.

Along with Bob, Indy 500 drivers Johnny Rutherford and Bobby Rahal and Unlimited Hydroplane boat racing champion (pilot of *Miss Budweiser*) Chip Hanauer made up the professional field. There were thirteen celebrities entered, including Steven Baldwin, singers Peter Cetera and Dwight Yoakam, TV broadcasters Jack Arute and Paul Page, football star Larry Csonka, and a young and pretty radio personality named Monica Brooks. Long before the event, all of the celebrities attended the Fast Lane Racing School, run by Danny McKeever. McKeever was also in charge of the celebrity event in Long Beach.

Everything seemed to be going along nicely as the time for the big race approached. Of course there was some good-natured kidding between the competitors. Steven Baldwin had T-shirts made up with a logo that said "We're Gunning for Hanna," with Hannah's name purposely misspelled. Rutherford and Rahal ragged on Hannah with great enthusiasm. At breakfast before the race, Rutherford claimed he hadn't slept, that he'd just been lying awake all night worrying about racing Bob Hannah. Holding back laughter, Rutherford said, "When I called Rahal at 2:00 a.m., he said he couldn't sleep, either."

Hanauer and Hannah seemed to be new best friends at a dinner party the night before the race, spending time trading race stories. Race morning, however, there was a noticeable mood swing. Both Hanauer and Hannah had on their race faces. Match a guy who drives 200-mile-per-hour jet boats against someone who won seven national championships through sheer determination, and you can see a problem brewing. The race began and it seemed only minutes before the professionals had bridged the thirty-second gap enforced by the handicap start and were hunting down the celebrities like wolves would sheep. Rahal simply terrorized the field, mercilessly passing the hapless front runners with Rutherford, Hanauer, and Hannah in tow.

Above: Stephen Baldwin had some T-shirts printed. Too bad he can't spell. *TMP*

Opposite: In 1990, Bob Hannah was a participant in the Toyota Pro/Celebrity Race at the Long Beach Grand Prix. Although Hannah ran as a professional, he was a hit with the celebrities. *TMP*

Bob "Hurricane" Hannah
17
GOODYEAR
Suspension Techniques
DENSO SPARK PLUGS
DAECO RACING GASOLINE
SIMPSON RACE PRODUCTS
TOKICO
Dustin Nguyen

Quickly, the less experienced drivers became roadblocks and things started getting rough. Hanauer began an aggressive charge, forgetting he was racing non-professionals, not giving an inch to anyone. Hannah watched as Hanauer spun the helpless Monica Brooks going into a tight corner. To Chip it was just racing; she was in the way. To Hannah it was one of those uncalled for hits he never took sitting down as a racer. At the next corner Hannah returned the favor to Hanauer, spinning him and producing major sheet metal damage on both Toyota Celica race cars; nothing personal, stuff happens in racing, was Hannah's conclusion. He then went on to set the fastest lap of the race.

Rahal won the event, Baldwin took second place, and the Hurricane finished third. However, the growing friendship between Hannah and Hanauer was out the window—officials had to separate the two after the race. Toyota Public Relations surveyed the wreckage and concluded it was all part of the game. Danny McKeever threw his hands in the air as frustration overcame him.

Bob's Toyota Celica as it was when given to him. Within hours, Hannah crashed it into Chip Hanauer's car, and the two almost came to blows. *TMP*

The Hurricane doesn't spend all of his time riding in the dirt or flying airplanes, he likes to do a little street riding when the opportunity presents itself. These days, Hannah rides a Harley, but in 1986, a Suzuki was the ride of choice. Note the high-tech protective footwear. *TMP*

9

NO MORE STARTING GATES: LIVING HAPPILY EVER AFTER

EPILOGUE

According to Brian Lunniss the Hurricane was the hardest-working rider he had ever known. Says Brian, "In the years Bob rode for Honda, it was the heyday of the works bike, so I would build a bike exactly the way he wanted it to be. It fit his style to perfection." *TMP*

A FEW LAST WORDS FROM THE PROFESSOR

GARY BAILEY

Before I retired from actual competition, Bob Hannah hit the scene. The first time I watched Bob Hannah ride, I was blown away. What blew me up was his intensity and desire to win. He wasn't about style; he was about speed and winning. Hannah wanted first place; nothing else mattered. He did things on a bike that couldn't be done. I remember one time at a National Outdoor in Atlanta, Bob fell down in the first lap. He held the clutch in and jumped back on the bike and took off after the pack. About halfway through the moto, I said to myself, "Crap, he's going to win this thing," and he did.

As a young rider, Bob was never one to just hang out with the other competitors. If he said anything it would be, "Hey, hi, see ya. I never really liked ya anyway."

In the case of my son, David, when he became a teammate at Honda, Hannah took a real liking to him. I think it was because David was really down to earth. He wasn't cocky or arrogant. In fact, David would tell me he remembered standing in line and waiting to get an autograph from Bob when he rode for Yamaha. Although David had been riding for a long time and had grown up at my motocross school, he still learned from Bob.

I don't think they ever had a harsh word as teammates.

There were a few times I got to go riding with Hannah and David when they rode for Honda, and I was always amazed at the things Bob could do and still remain upright. I tell the kids at my school all the time, "Hannah was the only rider I knew who would crash and, while he was crashing, would be making a plan for getting going after the hit and, at the same time, was trying not to crash in the first place."

A jublilant Bob Hannah in the middle of a crowd at Unadilla in New Berlin, New York. Although Unadilla was always the Hurricane's favorite track, victory had eluded him there until the USGP in 1986. Here he is being told he won the race after Johnny O'Mara ran out of gas. While it wasn't the way Hannah would have preferred to win, a Unadilla victory was so long in coming that it still felt pretty good. *Gary Bailey*

Two great champions, David Bailey (left) and Bob Hannah (right). Bailey was teammate to Hannah at Honda and showed his great ability by winning the 1983 AMA 250cc Outdoor National Championship and the 1983 Supercross title. Sadly, David's career was cut short by a terrible accident. Bailey now fights to help those with spinal cord injuries. *Hannah*

INDEX

100 Years of Harley-Davidson, 22
AAA Midget, 170
Aldana, Dave, 24
Ali, Muhammad, 6
AMA
  District 37, 23
  Flat Track, 88
  Motorcycle Hall of Fame, 19
Amick, Bill, 25
Anaheim Stadium, 106, 107, 116, 120
Andrews, Mick, 24
Answer Products, 62, 63, 64, 110
Armstrong, Lance, 120, 139
Arnold, Dave, 6, 7, 43, 51, 52, 54, 55, 138, 139
Arute, Jack, 165
Ascot Park Raceway, 25
Bailey
  Bob, 23
  David, 6, 23, 33, 80, 102, 106, 108, 110, 112–117, 120, 138, 139, 173
  Gary, 23–25, 88, 92, 128, 173
Baja 1000, 51
Baker, Al, 11
Baldwin, Stephen, 165, 167
Barnett, Mark, 110, 113, 133
Bay Mare track, 24
Bell
  Helmets, 60, 61, 123
  Mike, 73, 79, 97, 113
  Ranger, 64
Bel-Ray Oil Company, 108
Berquist, Larry, 11
Bevo (Robert Forti), 61, 66, 78, 97–103
Blackwell, Mark, 25, 128
Blue Angels, The, 16, 157, 158
Bob Hannah Aviation, 146, 160
Bonneville Salt Flats, 22
Boone, Mickey, 50, 51
Bowen, Keith, 117
Boyko, Ken, 11, 12, 60, 61
Brando, Marlon, 22
Breker, Goat, 106
Brolin, James, 164
Brooks, Monica, 165, 167
Buchka, Bill, 7, 42, 43, 46, 47, 50–53, 55, 56, 66, 69, 70, 72, 88, 98
Bultaco, 63
Burgett, Rick, 35, 44, 45, 63, 72, 73
Burnworth, Scott, 115
Bush Hawk, 155
Button, Bob, 145, 158
Callaway, Mel, 37
Can-Am series, 42, 43
Cantaloupi, Donnie, 98
Carlsbad track, 24, 30
Carmichael, Ricky, 33, 97
Castaic track, 24
Castle Rock, 115, 117
Catalina Grand Prix, 20, 22, 23
Catalina Island Company, 23
Cessna 210, 14
Cetera, Peter, 165
Chandler, Danny, 50, 123, 139
Clark, Kenny, 76
CMC (Continental Motosport Club), 35
Cole, Eddie, 62–66, 110
Conrad, Pete, 164
Cox, Dennis, 129
Croft, Tommy, 35, 73
Csonka, Larry, 165
Cycle magazine, 129
Cycle World magazine, 23, 129
DeCoster, Roger, 6, 7, 24, 41, 44, 46, 52, 61, 68, 97, 130, 138, 139
DeFeo, Sonny, 25
DeSoto, John, 24, 34
Despain, Dave, 88
DG Performance Specialties, 11, 35, 60, 61
Dirt Bike magazine, 129
Dirt Diggers, 24
DiStefano, Tony, 25, 41, 49, 66, 69, 70, 138
Dory, Joe, 32
Dudek, Don, 43
Dye, Edison, 24
Earnhardt, Dale Sr., 15
Eastwood, Clint, 164
Ekins, Bud, 23
Ellis, Jimmy, 12, 42, 43
Elway, John, 164
Englund, Ario, 54
Escape Country, 30
ESPN, 95, 145, 152
Evans, Walker, 12
Eyvind Boyesen, 85, 145
Fast Lane Racing School, 165
Felts, Jim, 72
Ferrari 308, 64
FIM (Federation Internationale de Motocyclimse), 52
Flanders, Bruce, 88
Florida Winter Series, 63, 130, 139
Formula One boat racing, 124, 145
Foyt, A. J., 15
French Grand Prix, 145
Galloping Gooses, 23
Gianatsis, Jim, 129
Gillman family, 152
Glick, Shav, 129
GlobalFlyer, 160
Glover, Broc, 50, 54–56, 70, 72, 73, 76, 79, 113, 137
Golden State series, 79, 116, 117
Good, Terry, 42, 47, 50
Goodwin, Mike, 13, 88
Goodyear Tires, 60, 61
Great Outdoors, 145
Gregory, John, 64
Grossi, Billy, 43, 52, 53, 56, 138
Gurney, Dan, 164
Hackman, Gene, 164
Hailwood, Mike, 152
Hallman, Torsten, 24
Hanauer, Chip, 162, 165, 167
Hangtown track, 8, 43, 50, 51, 61, 65, 82, 110–112, 120, 121, 124
Hannah
  Barbara, 28, 32
  Bill, 28–30, 32, 41, 129
  Mel, 28, 29, 41, 129
  Racing Products, 64, 79
  Tammy (Dory), 28, 29, 31–33, 60
  Terri, 153–155, 161
Hansen, Donnie, 138, 139
Harlow, Gary, 11, 12, 35–37, 60, 61
Hart, Tim, 50, 51
Hells Angels, 23
Henderson track, 120
Herd, Steve, 34
Hickey, Vic, 15
Hicks, Jeff, 76, 77, 79–87, 114, 123, 146
Higgins, Barry, 25
Hi-Point riding boots, 88, 89, 97
Hodaka 90, 29
Hodoka Ace, 25
Honda
  55, 29
  Elsinore 125cc, 51
  Type-1, 55
  Type-2 125, 54, 55
  Team, 6, 7, 51, 92, 114, 126, 134, 138
Hope, Bob, 24
Hopetown track, 24
Howerton, Kent, 74, 75, 97, 133, 142
Huffman, Larry, 13, 15, 87, 88, 92, 98, 106
Husqvarna 250cc, 34
Indian Dunes Motorcycle Park, 30, 63
Indianapolis 500, 106, 129, 146, 165, 170, 171
Inter-Am series, 24
J&R Expansion Chambers, 30
Jenner, Bruce, 164
Jennings, Jeff, 43
Jim Russell Driving School, 129, 147
John Penton Motorcycles, 88
John Wayne Winchester Commemorative, 97
Johnson, Rick, 79, 83, 95, 97, 112, 113, 115, 120, 123, 139
Jones, Gary, 128
Jones, Parnelli, 12, 15, 164
Kanegae, Dennis, 40–42
Kariya, Mark, 129
Karsmakers, Pierre, 24, 36, 43, 97
Keller, Jo-Jo, 118
Kiedrowski, Mike, 51
Kingdome track, 81, 108, 109
Koyama, Tosh, 35
Kudaiski, Don, 52
Kuhn, Fran, 129
Lackey, Brad, 25, 63, 92, 95, 128
Laguna Seca track, 69, 147
Lake Elsinore track, 24
Lake Mead, 77
LaPorte, Danny, 43, 50, 51, 56
Lawson, Eddie, 152
Lechein, Ron, 113
Leonard, Joe, 152
Life magazine, 22
Limbaugh, Rush, 155
Lindstrom, Gunnar, 24

Lockheed Aircraft, 28
Long Beach Grand Prix, 165
Los Angeles Coliseum, 12, 37, 43, 84, 85, 97, 120, 140
Los Angeles Times, 129
Lunniss, Brian, 12, 79, 80, 82, 101, 103, 106, 108–110, 112–116, 120, 121, 123, 137–140, 143, 172
Madigan, Darlene, 12, 95, 106, 108, 109, 116
Madigan, Tom, 95
Maiers, Larry, 19, 87–97, 99, 101–103, 125, 145, 152
Mann, Dick, 24
Marvin, Lee, 23
Matheson, Al, 23
McCarty, Keith, 11, 19, 25, 54, 66, 69, 70, 79, 90, 98, 99, 130, 136–138
McDougal, Bruce, 51
McGrath, Jeremy, 33, 97
McKee, Mick, 30, 34
McKeever, Danny, 165, 167
McQueen, Steve, 12
Mears, Rick, 15
Mears, Roger, 12, 15
Mexican 1000, 11, 15
Midland track, 51, 52
Mikkola, Heikki, 70, 97, 99
Miller, Dick, 129
Millville track, 116, 153, 155
Montana, Joe, 164
Moto Cross magazine, 129
Motocross Action magazine, 42, 55, 129
Motocross America, 25
Motocross des Nations, 13, 25, 33, 35, 46, 51, 70, 73, 85, 95, 99, 125, 128, 133, 145
Motorcycle Olympiad, 133
MotoWorld, 95, 145, 152
Murray, Jim, 129
Myerscough Machine Company, 60
Nanni, Dario, 64
National Air Races, 129, 158
NHRA, 66
Nillsson, Gunnar, 11
Nilsson, Nils Arne, 43
Northwest Backcountry Aircraft, 146
O'Mara, Johnny, 6, 83, 95, 102, 110, 116–118, 138, 139, 173
Off-Road magazine, 11, 112
Outdoor Nationals
  125cc, 7, 36, 41–44, 46, 50–57, 63, 69, 70, 92, 98, 99, 102, 130
  250cc, 7, 8, 13, 25, 38, 45, 56, 65, 66, 69, 70, 72, 74, 75, 80, 82, 83, 98, 104, 106, 111, 112, 114–116, 120, 121, 130, 135, 142, 173
  500cc, 45, 51, 56, 63, 69, 70, 130
P-47 aircraft, 158
P-51 Mustang, 19, 129, 145, 158–161
Page, Paul, 165
Paris-to-Dakar Rally, 51
Patrick, Danica, 164
Penton, John, 88, 128
Piper 250 Comanche, 15
Pitts Special Aerobatic, 16, 77, 95, 152
Pomeroy, Jim, 25, 44, 92, 128
Popular Cycling magazine, 11
Preston Petty Fenders, 69
Price, David, 158
Rahal, Bobby, 162, 164, 167
Rahier, Gaston, 53
Reagan, Ronald, 145
Red Bud track, 51, 52, 61, 88, 92, 114, 136
Reid, Warren, 50, 54, 56
Reno Air Races, 145, 161
Retton, Mary Lou, 164
Reyes, Steve, 66
Riverside Raceway, 129
Robert, Joel, 24
Roberts, J. N., 11
Roberts, Kenny, 41, 72
Roeslet, Larry, 11
Rutan, Burt, 160
Rutherford, Johnny, 162, 165
Saddleback Park track, 24, 25, 28, 30, 40, 41, 72, 74, 75, 102, 112, 116, 133, 138
San Diego track, 120
Santa Monica Museum of Flying, 158
Santa Paula Airport, 158
Satan's Slaves, 22
Savitski, John, 50, 51, 56, 79, 90, 98, 99
Scaled Composites Corporation, 160
Schick, Pete, 37, 40, 41
Schiedler, Ed, 51
Scott Goggles, 60, 61
Scott USA, 97, 101
Seaman, Rick, 129
Semics, Gary, 25, 128
Shiganoya, T., 37, 142
Silverdome track, 70, 92, 93, 113
Slovak, Mira, 150, 157, 158
Smith, Malcolm, 11, 17
Smith, Marty, 7, 11, 35, 41–43, 46, 47, 49–56, 92, 95
Sorenson, Warren, 120
SpaceShipOne, 160
Spencer, Jeff, 114, 120, 139
Stackable, Steve, 43, 45
Staten, Rex, 34
Stewart, James, 33, 97
Sugia, Yoshifumo, 53
Sun, Chuck, 35, 73
Super Bowl of Motocross, 43
Super Moto Cross magazine, 129
Supercross, 12, 13, 17, 45, 61, 70, 72, 77, 80, 83–85, 88, 89, 92, 93, 95, 97, 98, 101, 104, 106–108, 110, 113, 114, 116, 118, 120, 123, 130, 134, 135, 138–140, 142, 145, 149, 173
Suzuki 125cc, 95
Suzuki, Team, 6, 24, 46, 48, 58
Tangerine Bowl stadium, 114
Thompson, Mickey, 15
Tibblen, Rolf, 36
Toyota
  Celica, 167
  Grand Prix, 164
  Motor Sales, 164
  Pro/Celebrity Grand Prix, 124, 162–167
  Public Relations, 164, 167
Tracy Party Ice, 15
Trans-AMA series, 25, 45, 46, 56, 63, 68, 70, 72, 74, 78, 98, 130, 134, 137
Tripes, Marty, 97, 99, 101, 133–135
Triumph 650cc, 24, 28
Trophée des Nations, 99, 133
TT Scrambles, 23, 24
Turner, Danny, 43, 56
Unadilla track, 19, 76, 88, 89, 94, 95, 124, 145, 170, 173
United States Navy, 16, 158
Unlimited Hydroplane, 165
Unser, Al, 164
Unser, Johnny, 146
USA Network, 95
USGP, 52–54, 116, 145, 173
Valencia Sport Group, 63
Valenta, Tracy, 15
Valley Cycle Park, 30, 37
Vimond, Jacky, 124
Vonlossberg, Greg, 77
Voodoo, 145, 158–160
Vukovich, Bill, 170, 171
Ward, Jeff, 95, 113, 120, 129, 152
Washougal track, 117, 118
Wayne, John and Ethan, 97
Webb, Tom, 129
Weinert, Jimmy, 25, 41, 48, 49, 92, 97, 128, 133
Weisel, Jody, 129
West, Bill, 88
Westlake Village track, 24
Wild One, The, 22
Wise, Steve, 43, 52, 56
Wolsink, Gerrit, 24
Wynn, Keenan, 23
Yamaha
  125cc, 53, 54
  250cc, 41
  MX125, 29
  OW, 43
  OW26 500cc, 44
  OW27, 51–53
  OW39 500cc, 13
  Team, 45, 48, 51, 52, 75, 99, 130, 134, 142
  YZ125, 43
  YZ250, 40, 41, 69, 70
  YZ-80, 41
Yoakam, Dwight, 165